Poetic Meter
and
Poetic Form

Poetic Meter
and
Poetic Form

REVISED EDITION

PAUL FUSSELL
UNIVERSITY OF PENNSYLVANIA

Random House  *New York*

Revised Edition
9 8 7 6 5
Copyright © 1965, 1979 by Random House, Inc.
All rights reserved under International and Pan-American Copyright
Conventions. No part of this book may be reproduced in any form
or by any means, electronic or mechanical, including photocopying,
without permission in writing from the publisher.
All inquiries should be addressed to Random House, Inc.,
201 East 50th Street, New York, N.Y. 10022.
Published in the United States by Random House, Inc.,
and simultaneously in Canada by Random House of Canada Limited, Toronto.

LIBRARY OF CONGRESS CATALOGING IN PUBLICATION DATA

Fussell, Paul, 1924–
    Poetic meter and poetic form.

    Bibliography: p.
    Includes index.
    1.   English language—Versification. I.   Title.
PE1505.F78   1978   808.1   78–14548
ISBN 0–394–32120–0

Manufactured in the United States of America

Since this page cannot legibly accommodate all the copyright notices,
the following pages constitute an extension of the copyright page.

Typography by Lorraine Hohman

Cover design by Dana Kasarsky

Permissions Acknowledgments

Ezra Pound, "Hugh Selwyn Mauberley" from *Personae* by Ezra Pound. "Canto XI" and "Canto XXIII" from *The Cantos of Ezra Pound* by Ezra Pound. Copyright 1934 by Ezra Pound. By permission of New Directions and Faber and Faber, Ltd.

Henry Reed, "Lessons of the War: Naming of Parts" from *A Map of Verona*. By permission of Jonathan Cape Ltd.

Theodore Roethke, "Elegy for Jane" from *The Collected Poems of Theodore Roethke*. By permission of Doubleday & Company, Inc. and Faber and Faber, Ltd.

Margot Ruddock, "Autumn, Crystal Eye" from *Lemon Tree* by Margot Ruddock. By permission of J. M. Dent & Sons, Ltd.

Christopher Smart, from *Jubilate Agno* by Christopher Smart. By permission of Rupert Hart-Davis, Ltd./Granada Publishing Ltd.

Dylan Thomas, "The force that through the green fuse drives the flower" from *The Collected Poems of Dylan Thomas* by Dylan Thomas. Copyright 1939 by New Directions Publishing Corporation. By permission of New Directions, J. M. Dent & Sons, Ltd. and the Trustees for the Copyrights of the late Dylan Thomas.

Henry Van Dyke, "America for Me" from *The Works of Henry Van Dyke* by Henry Van Dyke. By permission of Charles Scribner's Sons.

Richard Wilbur, "Junk" from *Advice to a Prophet and Other Poems* by Richard Wilbur. "A Simile for Her Smile" from *Ceremony and Other Poems* by Richard Wilbur. By permission of Harcourt Brace Jovanovich and Faber and Faber, Ltd.

William Carlos Williams, "The Red Wheelbarrow" and "This is Just to Say" from *Collected Earlier Poems* by William Carlos Williams. Copyright 1938 by New Directions Publishing Corporation. "The Dance" from *Collected Later Poems* by William Carlos Williams. Copyright 1944 by William Carlos Williams. By permission of New Directions.

William Butler Yeats, "Among School Children," "A Prayer for My Son," "Sailing to Byzantium," and "The Tower" from *Collected Poems* by William Butler Yeats. Copyright 1928 by Macmillan Publishing Co., Inc., renewed 1956 by Georgie Yeats. "The Statues" and "Why Should Not Old Men Be Mad" from *Collected Poems* by William Butler Yeats. Copyright 1940 by Georgie Yeats, renewed 1968 by Bertha Georgie Yeats, Michael Butler Yeats and Anne Yeats. By permission of Macmillan Publishing Co., Inc.; M. B. Yeats; Miss Anne Yeats; and the Macmillan Co. of London and Basingstoke.

To My Brother

Foreword

The title of this book may suggest that it is designed as a latter-day *Gradus ad Parnassum* to teach aspiring writers to produce passable verses. It is not. It is intended to help aspiring readers deepen their sensitivity to the rhythmical and formal properties of poetry and thus heighten their pleasure and illumination as an appropriately skilled audience of an exacting art.

For this Revised Edition I have made corrections and additions throughout; sought additional examples; added an entirely new chapter on free verse; and brought up to date the Suggestions for Further Reading. Twelve years of teaching with the aid of this book have shown me some of its original defects of overstatement. I have tried to redress these, but I have not altered the generally traditional point of view, believing that the great classic majority of English and American poems deserve a fair shake on their own terms.

I want to thank the Research Council of Rutgers University for sympathetic and generous support. I must thank the Princeton University Press for permission to revise and include some of the materials I contributed to Alex Preminger's *Princeton Encyclopedia of Poetry and Poetics* (1965; enlarged edition, 1974). I am indebted to my friend and colleague C. F. Main for his suggestions. Chapter 5 has benefited from the criticism of Theodore Weiss. I owe a debt to Professors Edward Weismiller and the late W. K. Wimsatt for their help. I feel a special obligation to Professor Charles S. Holmes, late of Pomona College, under whose elegant tuition many years ago—we were reading *Paradise Lost*—I first learned how to delight in meter. And if my wife, Betty, will consult p. 112, she will find suggested in two lines there how indispensable she has always been to my enterprises.

P. F.

Contents

PART ONE

Poetic Meter

1

The Nature of Meter

"Rhythm *must* have meaning," Ezra Pound insisted in 1915. And he is right. The empirical study of poetry will convince us that meter is a prime physical and emotional constituent of poetic meaning. The great monuments of perception in English poetry—*Paradise Lost,* "The Rape of the Lock," *Songs of Innocence and Experience,* "The Rime of the Ancient Mariner," "Mauberley," "The Waste Land"—have constituted moments of metrical discovery: they all reveal an excitement with meter almost as an object of fundamental meaning in itself. Two modern poets have testified that to write poems is sometimes less to arrange ideas and assertions than to manipulate meters. W. H. Auden has said: "Every poet has his dream reader: mine keeps a look out for curious prosodic fauna like bacchics and choriambs." Asked by the editor of an anthology to choose two of his favorite poems and to give his reasons for choosing them, Auden wrote: "The first, 'In Due Season,' I choose because it is the only English poem since Campion written in accentual asclepiads; the second, 'Prologue at Sixty,' because I think the alliterative meter not badly handled." Themes and subjects for poems, Auden maintains, are less interesting to the real poet than technique, and "all my life," he says, "I have been more interested in poetic technique than anything else." And a comment of T. S. Eliot's can serve as a caution against the assumption that a poet's metrical decisions, because presumably instinctive and automatic, are somehow immune to criticism and even to analysis. Writing to Cleanth Brooks about an explication which Brooks had undertaken of one of his poems, Eliot observed: "Reading your essay made me feel . . . that I had been a great deal more ingenious than I had been aware of, because the conscious problems with which one is concerned in the actual writing are more those of a quasi musical nature, in the arrangement of metric and pattern, than of a conscious exposition of ideas." Which is to say that regardless of the amount and quality of intellectual and emotional analysis that precedes poetic composition, in the moment of composition itself the poet is most conspicuously performing as metrist. And the same principle holds for the reader: at the moment of his first apprehension of the poem he functions less as semanticist than as a more or less unwitting prosodist. It is the purpose of this book to help the reader to become, as prosodist, less unwitting.

When Boswell asked Johnson, "What is poetry?" Johnson answered: "Why, Sir, it is much easier to say what it is not. We all *know* what light is; but it is not easy to *tell* what it is." In the same way, everyone knows what meter is, but it is not easy to *tell* what it is. The first thing to say is that we know almost nothing about it, especially about how much of it is "in" the pattern of written words before us and how much "in" the reader's mind and musculature. We can say, however, that meter inheres in more or less regular linguistic rhythm; or we can say that talk about meter is a way of describing our awareness of those rhythmical patterns in poetic language which can be measured and formulated. Perhaps when we speak of meter we mean the "ideal" pattern which poetic rhythms approximate. That is, if meter is regarded as an ideal and thus invariable formal pattern, then rhythm moves toward meter the closer it approaches regularity and predictability.

Civilization is an impulse toward order; but high civilizations are those which operate from a base of order without at the same time denying the claims of the unpredictable and even the irrational. The impulse toward the metrical organization of assertions seems to partake of the more inclusive human impulse toward order. Meter is what results when the natural rhythmical movements of colloquial speech are heightened, organized, and regulated so that pattern—which means repetition—emerges from the relative phonetic haphazard of ordinary utterance. Because it inhabits the physical form of the words themselves, meter is the most fundamental technique of order available to the poet. The other poetic techniques of order—rhyme, line division, stanzaic form, and over-all structure—are all projections and magnifications of the kind of formalizing repetition which meter embodies. They are meter writ large.

Everyone knows that poetic meter, even when unskillfully managed, tends to produce a pleasant effect, but metrical theorists disagree vigorously about the reason for the universal popularity of metered compositions. According to some theorists (mostly rationalists), meter is pleasant because it focuses the reader's attention and refines his awareness. Thus to Coleridge meter tends "to increase the vivacity and susceptibility both of the general feelings and of the attention. . . . As a medicated atmosphere, or as a wine during animated conversation, [the expectations aroused by meter] act powerfully, though themselves unnoticed." According to other theorists (mostly romanticists), meter operates by inducing in the reader a state resembling hypnosis. Some argue that, since the beat in most accentual poetry is slightly faster than the normal heart beat, the apprehension of metered language physically exhilarates the hearer or reader: the heart beat, it is said, actually speeds up in an effort to "match" the slightly faster poetic rhythm. According to I. A. Richards, the effect of poetic rhythm is distinctly physiological and perhaps sexual. As he says, "Its effect is not due to our perceiving a pattern in something outside us, but to our becoming patterned ourselves. With every beat of the metre a tide of anticipation in us turns and swings. . . ." And he goes on to say: "We shall never understand metre so long as we ask, 'Why does temporal pattern so excite us?' and fail to realize that the pattern itself is a vast cyclic agitation spreading all over the body, a tide of excitement pouring through the channels of the mind." Coleridge may have meant something similar when he asserted that "The poet . . . brings the whole soul of man into activity."

The pleasure which universally results from foot tapping and musical time-beating does suggest that the pleasures of meter are essentially physical and as intimately connected with the rhythmic quality of our total experience as the similarly alternating and recurring phenomena of breathing, walking, or love-making. But the quality of the apprehender of meter determines the kinds of pleasure available from it: children and the unsophisticated receive from meter almost wholly physical pleasure, manifesting itself in foot tapping and head nodding. On the other hand, more experienced and sensitive readers probably derive much of their metrical pleasure from the high degree of rhetorical attention which meter demands ("Meter keeps the mind on the stretch," one critic has said), or from the intellectual and humanistic delight of witnessing order and containment being born out of chaos and flux. Medieval theories of meter, in fact, frequently assume that the pleasure man takes in meter is a simulacrum of the pleasure he takes in the principle of order and recurrence in a universe which itself would seem to be will and order incarnate.

When a poem is read aloud, its metrical effects are broadcast in the familiar currency of auditory impulses: the sounds and the pauses strike the ear in the normal way of sounds and silences, and the results lend themselves to notation by physicists and acoustic prosodists. But what happens when we, as we usually do, encounter a poem through silent, solitary reading? What is the nature of the rhythmical phenomena when our eyes rather than our lips or ears are doing the primary work? Everyone will consult his own experience to answer such questions accurately, but perhaps we can suggest that what happens is this: what we "hear" is a silent voice—our own—enunciating the words for the benefit of our listening muscular system. The "body swayed to music" of Yeats's "Among School Children" is a sort of emblem of the reader responding to silent metrical effects. A kind of motionless, silent dancing is what the reader does when he is responding metrically—as he must—to his own silent reading of a poem.

The word *meter* derives from the Greek term for "measure," and a good way to distinguish various metrical systems is to consider what is being "measured" or counted in each. Four metrical systems are generally distinguishable: the syllabic, the accentual (sometimes called "stress meter" or "strong stress meter"), the accentual-syllabic (sometimes called "syllable-stress"), and the quantitative.

Syllabic prosody measures only the number of syllables per line without regard to the stress of the syllables relative to each other. Poets and critics working in syllabic contexts sometimes use the term "numbers" as a synonym for "versification." Although stress does appear in lines of verse composed syllabically, it functions as a device of embellishment or rhetorical emphasis rather than as a criterion of the metrical skeleton of the line. Poetry in the Romance languages and in Japanese tends to be syllabic in construction because of the minor role which accent plays in those languages. From the period of the Restoration until about 1740, most English poetry tended to turn syllabic—perhaps influenced by French practice—but since that time syllabism has seldom been revived in English poetry except as a novelty. In the late nineteenth and early twentieth centuries Robert Bridges experimented with syllabic meter, and more recently W. H. Auden, Marianne Moore, Yvor Winters, Alan Stephens, Thom Gunn, and Donald Hall have composed on occasion syllabically. But despite sporadic successes, even these poets would probably agree that syllabism is not a natural measuring system in a language so Germanic and thus so accentual as English.

Indeed, when syllabic meter does produce engaging effects, they will often be found the result of a lurking system of stresses which the poet has not been able to wish away. In Bridges's "Cheddar Pinks," for example, the poet's design of writing alternating five- and six-syllable lines with stress used nonstructurally has been frustrated by the English language itself and by our own Anglo-Saxon instinct to hear stress, which prompts us to perceive a basis of two stresses per line:

> Mid the squander'd colour
> idling as I lay
> Reading the Odyssey
> in my rock garden
> I espied the cluster'd
> tufts of Cheddar pinks
> Burgeoning with promise
> of their scented bloom.

In a syllabic poem like Marianne Moore's "In Distrust of Merits" the quatrain which concludes the stanzas generally remains decently syllabic with the stresses falling apparently whimsically. For example:

> his ground in patience patience
>   patience, that is action or
> beauty', the soldier's defence
>   and hardest armor for

Here the pattern for the syllable count is seven, seven, seven, six. All goes well within this syllabic system until the climactic ending of the poem, where a major personal assertion rather than gentle comment is called for. It is interesting to watch the accents rising now from underground to take over the stanza and to shatter the syllabic surface as the passion and the commitment also rise:

> I inwardly did nothing.
>   O Iscariotlike crime!
> Beauty is everlasting
>   and dust is for a time.

It would seem that quiet description of Cheddar pinks or gently sardonic commentary on military ironies can contain itself sufficiently within syllabic versification. But in English, accent, like passion and murder, will out, and it will out the moment the poet, arrived at a climax, seizes all the techniques of prosodic reinforcement offered him by the conventions of the English language.

Another difficulty with syllabic meter in English is that in order to sense the shape of the poem the reader must halt unnaturally at line endings. The reader, who has naturally learned to measure language by stresses rather than by syllables, will find it all but impossible to grasp the metrical conformations of the syllabic poem without executing an elaborately unnatural pause at the end of each line.

Writing syllabic poems is difficult and reading them is fun, in a theoretical kind of way. But it is really stress that makes English poetry, and before examining accentual meter in English we should pause to consider just what stress or accent is. Here again we must proceed without much more certainty than saying that stress is the vocal emphasis with which a syllable is spoken—either aloud or silently—relative to the emphasis received by contiguous syllables. But to call stress "emphasis" is not to define it, and disagreement about the nature of stress is traditional in prosodic discussion. A spoken syllable manifests at least four phonetic qualities: pitch (highness or lowness on the musical scale), loudness, length (length of time consumed by the utterance of the syllable), and timbre or quality (that is, fuzziness, hoarseness, sharpness). Clearly when some of these phonetic qualities are emphasized we say that the syllable is accented, but we really do not know the answers to questions like these: Does an accented syllable have a higher pitch than an unaccented one? Is it louder? Has it a longer duration? Has it a unique timbre? Or is its emphatic characteristic the result of some sort of mysterious energy or "impulsion" which is not entirely accounted for by either pitch, loudness, length, or quality? There is little solid agreement on these questions among authorities, though even a very coarse sensibility can perceive that the line

> To me the meanest flower that blows can give

consists of alternating "accented" and "unaccented" syllables.

While in syllabic meter only the syllables are counted, in accentual meter only the accents are. Syllables may vary in number per line, it being assumed that three or four short syllables can be uttered in the same time that one or two long ones can. If syllabic meter seems naturally appropriate to Romance poetry, it is accentual meter which is the basis of most Germanic poetries —including Old English—and of most poems in Modern English in which the number of syllables varies from line to line. In the following lines by Yeats, for example, we find four stresses per line, although the number of syllables varies from seven to nine:

> Why should not old men be mad?
> Some have known a likely lad
> That had a sound fly-fisher's wrist
> Turn to a drunken journalist;
> A girl that knew all Dante once
> Live to bear children to a dunce;
> A Helen of social welfare dream,
> Climb on a wagonette to scream.

And in these lines of Auden's we find generally three stresses, with the number of syllables varying from six to eight:

> I sit in one of the dives
> On Fifty-second Street
> Uncertain and afraid
> As the clever hopes expire
> Of a low dishonest decade;
> Waves of anger and fear
> Circulate over the bright
> And darkened lands of the earth
> Obsessing our private lives.

Robert Frost has maintained that the contemporary poet has available only two meters, strict iambic and loose iambic. If accentual meters like Yeats's and Auden's are regarded as "loose iambic," we can begin to invoke the term "strict iambic" as the number of both accents and syllables becomes regularized—that is, as the accentual moves toward the accentual-syllabic.

In this third metrical system, both the accents and the syllables are measured and numbered, and the mensuration is often conceived of in terms of *feet,* that is, conventional patterns or units of stressed and unstressed syllables. In accentual-syllabic meter, variations in accent position, addition, or omission are more readily accepted than variations in the number of syllables per line. The result of this strictness is a metrical medium of some rigidity and inflexibility, but at the same time of considerable compressive power. The accentual-syllabic system is the general mode of versification employed by conservative prosodic practitioners in English: Spenser, Shakespeare, Milton, Dryden, Pope, Swift, and Johnson are examples. Accentual-syllabic meter seems to be fashionable during ages interested in classical rhetoric and committed to a sense of human limitation and order. Of all metrical systems in English, the accentual-syllabic is the most hostile by nature to impulse, irregularity, and unrestrained grandiosity. It seems all but impossible to transmit impressions of hysteria or the frantic within a strict accentual-syllabic versification: a weighty judiciousness is the tone most commonly associated with accentual-syllabism. The following example from Swift's "The Beasts' Confession to the Priest" exemplifies both the accentual and the syllabic limitations. The accents per line are four, the syllables eight:

> Creatures of ev'ry Kind but ours
> Well comprehend their nat'ral Powers;
> While We, whom *Reason* ought to sway,
> Mistake our Talents ev'ry Day.

As in this example, the presence of syncope (the conventional omission of presumably supernumerary syllables: *ev'ry; nat'ral*) is generally a sign that a strict accentual-syllabism is being regarded as the prosodic vehicle. Another example, this time from Gray's "Elegy." Here the accents are five per line, the syllables ten. The stanza closes rigidly around its materials, containing them with as much formality as the storied urn itself holds its inert contents:

> Can storied urn or animated bust
> Back to its mansion call the fleeting breath?
> Can Honour's voice provoke the silent dust,
> Or Flatt'ry soothe the dull, cold ear of death?

Quantitative meter, finally, measures durational rather than accentual feet; each foot, that is, consists of "long" and "short" rather than "accented" and "unaccented" syllables. Most Sanskrit, Greek, and Roman poems tend to be written quantitatively, and there have been many attempts (especially during the Renaissance) to compose English verse according to principles of duration rather than accent. Edmund Spenser, for example, in his *"Iambicum Trimetrum,"* imitates the iambic trimeter (i.e., hexameter) of classical poetry:

> Unhappy verse, the witness of my unhappy state,
> Make thyself flutt'ring wings of thy fast flying
> Thought, and fly forth unto my love, wheresoever she be:
>
> Whether lying restless in heavy bed, or else
> Sitting so cheerless at the cheerful board, or else
> Playing alone careless on her heavenly virginals.

Inspired by the theorizing of one William J. Stone, author of *On the Use of Classical Metres in English* (1898), Robert Bridges also experimented with quantitative English verse. Here, in "Wintry Delights," addressed to Lionel Johnson, he imitates the classical heroic hexameter:

Now in wintry delights, and long fireside meditation,
'Twixt studies and routine paying due court to the Muses,
My solace in solitude, when broken roads barricade me
Mudbound, unvisited for months with my merry children,
Grateful t'ward Providence, and heeding a slander against me
Less than a rheum, think of me today, Dear Lionel, and take
This letter as some account of Will Stone's versification.

But just as a syllabic poet's ambitions seem always to invite defeat from the force of English accent, so attempts to organize English lines according to quantitative feet risk awkwardness and self-consciousness. The English language is so heavily accented that no other of its characteristics but accent seems to furnish a basis for meter. Bridges himself has testified to the strenuous difficulty of thinking and feeling in quantities instead of in accents, and his experience suggests that a meter customary in a given language has become customary precisely because it measures the most conspicuous phonetic characteristic of that language.

Meter, one of the primary correlatives of meaning in a poem, can "mean" in at least three ways. First, all meter, by distinguishing rhythmic from ordinary statement, objectifies that statement and impels it toward a significant formality and even ritualism. This ritual "frame" in which meter encloses experience is like the artificial border of a painting: like a picture frame, meter reminds the apprehender unremittingly that he is not experiencing the real object of the "imitation" (in the Aristotelian sense) but is experiencing instead that object transmuted into symbolic form. Meter is thus a primary convention of artifice in poetry, like similar indispensable conventions (the palpably artificial stone flesh of statues, for example) in the other arts. The second way a meter can "mean" is by varying from itself: as we shall see, departures from metrical norms powerfully reinforce emotional effects. And third, meters can mean by association and convention. Because of its associations with certain kinds of statements and feelings, a given meter tends to maintain a portion of its meaning, whether symbolic sounds are attached to it or not. In the limerick, for example, the very pattern of short anapestic lines is so firmly associated with light impudence or indecency that a poet can hardly write in anything resembling this measure without evoking smiles. To "translate" a limerick into, say, iambic tetrameter, is to drain off the comedy: we must conclude that a great deal of the comedy inheres by now in the meter alone.

Similarly, triple meters (based on anapestic or dactylic feet) seem inevitably to have something vaguely joyous, comical, light, or superficial about them. In "Retaliation," Oliver Goldsmith makes the whimsical associations of triple meter work for him:

> To make out the dinner full certain I am
> That Ridge is anchovy, and Reynolds is lamb;
> That Hickey's a capon, and by the same rule,
> Magnanimous Goldsmith a gooseberry fool.

In "The Poplar-Field," on the other hand, William Cowper, like Longfellow in "Evangeline," unwittingly allows the whimsical associations of triple meter to work against him:

> My fugitive years are all hasting away,
> And I must ere long lie as lowly as they,
> With a turf on my breast, and a stone at my head,
> Ere another such grove shall arrive in its stead.

On the other hand, William Carlos Williams happily exploits the associations of triple meter in "The Dance":

> In Breughel's great picture, The Kermess,
> the dancers go round, they go round and
> around, the squeal and the blare and the
> tweedle of bagpipes. . . .

So, with an impressive delicacy and fineness, does Henry Reed in "Naming of Parts," where a fatuous military instructor delivers his lesson in rifle nomenclature:

> To-day we have naming of parts. Yesterday,
> We had daily cleaning. And to-morrow morning,
> We shall have what to do after firing. But to-day,
> To-day we have naming of parts. . . .

Since ordinary people, and least of all noncommissioned officers, do not speak metrically, to present them speaking metrically is to transform them from creatures of nature into creatures of art. And when it is the poet's voice that we hear speaking metrically, the meter announces or implies his vatic role, just as meter tends to invest with a mysterious air of authority and permanence the words that assume its patterns. The strange power of meter to burnish the commonplace has tempted some people to regard metrical patterns as Platonic forms, themselves inherently and permanently beautiful, forms which the poet perceives as if by special illumination and toward which he constantly urges the rhythms of his own utterance.

If, like some Platonists, one regards regular meter as a kind of ideal, then one becomes extraordinarily sensitive to those places in the poem where the "sense" pattern of the language rhythm lies at some distance from the normal or "base" abstract rhythm of the metrical scheme. Prosodists and critics who have attended closely to this frequent distance between a poem's ideal and real meter have promulgated a theory of prosodic "tension": these theorists hold that one of the important sources of metrical power and pleasure is this perpetual tension between perfect and imperfect, or between general and particular, metrical patterns. The perpetual tension between the theoretical meter and the actual rhythms in a poem constitutes a sort of play or suspension between opposites, which may remind us of the aesthetics of Coleridge.

One complication to be kept in mind when we are dealing with meter is this: different kinds of poems use meter in different ways. Except for some of its most obvious offices, for example, it is apparent that meter does not do the same things in lyric that it does in poetic drama, where it helps actors memorize lines; nor does it do the same things in narrative poetry that it does in satiric. In "Thirty Days Hath September" and in the metered genealogies of epic, the function of meter is largely mnemonic; in a poem like "Kubla Khan" its function is musical and hypnotic; in something like the "Essay on Man" it is oratorical and analytically pedagogic. Different metrical values attach not only to the several modes of poetry (lyric, narrative, dramatic, satiric) but also to the several kinds (elegy, song, sonnet, ode). Thus what is merit in a limerick is a disaster in a sonnet. The kind of meter which sustains a long performance like "The Prelude" is likely to be too diffuse for a short one like "The World Is Too Much with Us." There is one perfect meter for "The Love Song of J. Alfred Prufrock" and another for "Mauberley": they should not be the same. We could do worse than agree with Pound when he says, "I believe in an absolute rhythm, a rhythm, that is, in poetry which corresponds exactly with the emotion or shade of emotion to be expressed."

John Hollander has spoken of "the metrical contract" which every poet undertakes with his reader from the first few words of a poem. Given the nature of each metrical contract, the reader tends to *do* certain things and not others as he reads. I. A. Richards has emphasized likewise the way the reader's response is determined and governed by the first lines of any poem. He says: "Just as the eye reading print unconsciously expects the spelling to be as usual, and the fount of type to remain the same, so the mind after reading a line or two of verse . . . prepares itself ahead for any one of a number of possible sequences, at the same time negatively incapacitating itself for others." And emphasizing that meter is illusion, and often illusion created more by the mind of the reader than by the pen of the writer, Richards concludes: "The effect produced by what actually follows [in the poem] depends very closely upon this unconscious preparation and consists largely of the further twist which it gives to expectancy."

What Richards is implying is that the reader's experience of meter is a phenomenon of which only the hints and promptings are provided by the actual rhythm of the poetic words. That is, the apprehender's mind and psyche and even physique tend to read meter into language in order to achieve their own organizational satisfactions. It is easy to test this premise by our own experience. The ticking of a clock constitutes an unvaried succession of regular sounds: when no one is listening, the clock goes *tick, tick, tick, tick* all day long. But let a human ear approach, and the clock goes *tick, tock, tick, tock,* and the ticking now "becomes" rhythmical because the listening ear wants it to be.

Consider now the following lines from the beginning of William Blake's "The Chimney Sweeper" (*Songs of Innocence*) :

> When my mother died I was very young,
> And my father sold me while yet my tongue
> Could scarcely cry, " 'weep! 'weep! 'weep! 'weep!"

Here the poet has so contracted that the reader refuses to consider the four *'weep*'s as a series of sounds equally stressed (contrast the reader's very different treatment of King Lear's "Then
kill, kill, kill, kill, kill, kill!"); instead, the reader shapes the
four *'weep*'s into two iambic groups and pauses between the two
groups. But if the *'weep*'s were removed from their context, the
metrical contract would be abrogated, and the reader would give
them equal stress as he does Lear's *kill*'s. Such is the authority of
the reader's lust for rhythm, once the poet who is in charge has
indicated that it is time for it to be unleashed and satisfied.

According to John Crowe Ransom, a poem is an organism like
a person, and, like a coherent person, the poem approaches to
merit and even to virtue when its head, its heart, and its feet are
all cooperating economically. The emphasis that we are going to
bring to the feet ought not to seduce us into an overemphasis.
It is true that great poems are great metrical achievements. But
great metrical achievement alone does not make great poetry. A
poet like Robert Bridges is an example of how little mere technical skill in versification—and his is a large and admirable skill
—will in the long run serve to redeem and make permanent a
poetry without any compelling intellectual or emotional impulse.

2

The Technique of Scansion

Scansion, which can be defined as any system of representing more or less conventional poetic rhythms by visual symbols for purposes of metrical analysis and criticism, does not make rhythm: it reveals and simplifies it by translating it from a temporal into a spatial dimension. By giving a critic a clear visual representation of the metrical situation in a poem, scansion becomes an elementary tool of criticism. If the tool is used clumsily and unimaginatively, the criticism will be primitive; but if the tool is used with devotion and sensitivity, the criticism has a good chance of coming to grips with matters of fundamental poetic value.

The practice of scansion derives, unfortunately, from the techniques of scholarship in the classical languages. This derivation has tended to invest the act of scansion with an air of the doctrinaire, the prescriptive, and the pedantic; for when a classical scholar scans some Greek or Latin verse, he *knows* what pattern the poet is following—or ought to be following—and keeps his eye peeled for "false quantities" or other blemishes indicating that the poet has neglected his metrical business. Our practice in scanning English poetry must be very different, partly because we shall be attending largely to an accentual or an accentual-syllabic rather than a quantitative poetry, and partly because English poetry employs quite different artistic principles from those of classical verse: it engages in much bolder and much more expres-

sive variations from metrical norms than classical poetry. Indeed,
it is to locate and interpret and finally to value these variations,
rather than to reprehend them, that we scan at all.

Prosodists use one of three systems of signs for scanning English
verse: the graphic, the musical, and the acoustic. In graphic scansion, which is the kind we shall be using, the reader affixes the
symbol ‿ to syllables which, in their context, are unstressed; he
uses the symbol ´ to indicate syllables which, in context, are
stressed. A division between poetic feet is indicated by /. A
caesura, or metrical pause, is indicated by ||. In musical scansion,
on the other hand, eighth notes may be used to represent unstressed syllables, and quarter or half notes to represent stressed
syllables of varying weights. Caesuras are sometimes indicated by
musical rests of various lengths. Musical scansion does have the
advantage of representing more accurately than graphic certain
delicate differences in degree of stress: it is obvious that an English line has more than two prosodic kinds of syllables in it, and
yet graphic scansion, preferring convenience to absolute accuracy,
seems to give the impression that any syllable in a line is either
clearly stressed or clearly unstressed. But musical scansion has
perhaps a greater disadvantage than this kind of oversimplifica-
tion: it is not only complex, but even worse tends to imply that
poetry follows musical principles closer than it does, an assumption that can lead to all sorts of misapprehensions not only of
rhythmical patterns but of total poetic meanings. The third
method of scansion, the acoustic, translates poetic sounds into the
marks on graph paper produced by such machines as the kymo-
graph and the oscillograph. Like musical scansion, this system has
the advantage of accuracy, especially in its representations of
many of the empirical phenomena of verse when it is actually
spoken aloud; its disadvantages are its complexity, its novelty,
and its incapacity to deal with rhythms which no speaker may
enunciate but which every silent reader feels. Musical scansion
may do no harm to those already learned in music and musical
theory; acoustic scansion may be useful to the linguist and the
scientist of language; but graphic scansion is best for those who
aspire to become not merely accurate readers but also intelligent
critics of English poetry.

In learning to perform graphic scansion of a line or group of
lines, the reader first marks stressed and unstressed syllables, *not*

according to any preconceived pattern, but according to the degree of rhetorical emphasis residing in the syllables. A good way to begin is to mark a prose sentence, thus: Thĕ ŏnly úsefŭl ĕxpĕctátĭon thăt ă réadĕr căn bríng tŏ ă póĕm ĭs thăt ĭt wĭll bĕ ĭn cértăin wáys ŭníque, ă thíng ĭn ĭtsélf. Having marked a prose sentence with regard only to the relative force of its various syllables in projecting its meaning and emphasis, we proceed to a stanza of poetry (here, from Edward Fitzgerald's *Rubaiyat*) and do the same:

Ĭ sómetĭmes thínk thăt névĕr blóws sŏ réd

Thĕ Róse ăs whére sóme búrĭed Cáesăr bléd;

Thăt éverÿ Hÿăcĭnth thĕ Gárdĕn wéars

Drópt ĭn hĕr láp frŏm sóme ónce lóvelÿ héad.

Notice that in scanning we mark according to the sound of words, not according to their appearance on the page: thus in the third line here, we mark *everÿ* rather than *évĕrÿ*, for that, whether correct or incorrect, is the way we actually say the word. The syllabic regularity in Fitzgerald's lines—each line has ten syllables—as well as the more or less regular placement of stresses suggests that the stanza is written in accentual-syllabic meter, and that hence it is appropriate to invoke the concept of poetic feet.

A poetic foot is a measurable, patterned, conventional unit of poetic rhythm. Because the idea of the foot has been imported into modern accentual-syllabic scansion from classical quantitative practice, quarrels about its nature and even its existence have been loud and long since the Renaissance. Most authorities would agree that if we are going to use the concept of the foot to describe the rhythmic norm of poetic lines, then the foot consists of one stressed syllable and one or two unstressed syllables. The poetic line in a more or less regular composition, traditionalists would maintain, consists of a number of feet from one to eight. By convention, the feet are conceived of as roughly of the same kind, although variations, produced by the "substitution" of different feet, are not only permissible but desirable so long as these substitutions do not efface for long the repeated pattern of the prevailing or dominant kind of foot, which establishes a "grid"—like the steady rhythmic beat in jazz—against which departures are audible as "syncopation."

The following are the most common "base" feet in English:

iamb (iambus) ; iambic, as in   dĕstróy

anapest (anapaest) ; anapestic   ĭntĕrvéne

trochee; trochaic   tópsў

dactyl; dactylic   mérrĭlў

And the following, although obviously not encountered as base feet, are frequently used for substitution:

spondee; spondaic   húm-drúm

pyrrhic   the sea/sŏn ŏf/mists

Iambic and anapestic feet are called—misleadingly—ascending or rising feet; trochaic and dactylic are known as descending or falling. A poem written prevailingly in iambic or anapestic feet is said to be in ascending or rising rhythm: the rhythm is so called because the reader is presumed to feel, in each foot, an "ascent" from a relatively unstressed syllable to a relatively stressed one. The term is useful only if we keep in mind that it has no metaphoric or symbolic value: ascending rhythm does not, in itself, transmit a feeling of aspiration, levity, or cheer, nor does descending rhythm—generated by prevailing trochees or dactyls—necessarily transmit illusions of falling nor emotions of depression or gloom.

In addition to classifying feet as ascending or descending, we can classify them as duple or triple: two-syllable feet like iambs and trochees are duple feet; three-syllable, like anapests and dactyls, triple. To exemplify poetic feet by single words, as above, is of course to distort their nature: foot divisions do not necessarily correspond to word divisions. Actually, the foot is rather like a musical bar in that both foot and bar are arbitrary abstract units of measure which do not necessarily coincide with the phrasal units on which they are superimposed. The difference between foot and bar is that the bar always begins with a stress.

Because the concept of the foot is an abstraction, we will never encounter a pure example of any of the standard feet. "For that matter," as Hugh Kenner says, "you will never encounter a round face, though the term is helpful; and if the idea of a circle had never been defined for you, you might not be clearly aware of how a round face differs from a long one, even though the existence of some sort of difference is evident to the eye. The term 'iambic foot' has the same sort of status as the term 'round face.' " Although we will probably never meet a really pure spondee or pyrrhic, in which the two syllables are of exactly the same weight, there would seem to be no need for such overscrupulous formulations as the terms "pseudo-spondee" or "false spondee," which suggest that our work as scansionists and critics ought to be more objective and accurate than of course it ever can be. The goal of what we are doing is enjoyment: an excessive refinement of terms and categories may impress others but it will probably not help us very much to appreciate English poetic rhythms.

The terminology of the poetic feet derives from classical quantitative prosody, and this too has been a source of misunderstanding and even hostility among readers of English, for in ancient poetry rhythmical usages are generally much more regular and predictable than in English poetry, where "substitutions" are governed by instinct, whim, or taste rather than by rule. Although it is not often necessary to invoke any more than the six feet indicated above in describing the rhythm of an English line, it does no harm to be acquainted with the following feet, all of which are to be found in Greek or Latin poetry (where, of course, duration of syllables rather than stress determines the pattern):

amphibrach   ⌄ ´ ⌄

antispast   ⌄ ´ ´ ⌄

bacchic   ⌄ ´ ´

choriamb   ´ ⌄ ⌄ ´

cretic   ´ ⌄ ´

epitrite   ⌄ ´ ´ ´

(called first, second, third, or fourth epitrite according to the position of the short syllable)

ionic a majore   ´ ´ ˘ ˘

ionic a minore   ˘ ˘ ´ ´

paeon   ´ ˘ ˘ ˘

(called first, second, third, or fourth paeon according to the position of the long syllable)

mollossus   ´ ´ ´

tribrach   ˘ ˘ ˘

Returning now to our *Rubaiyat* stanza: after ascertaining whether the rhythm in general is ascending or descending, we mark the feet, making certain that the end of each line corresponds with the end of a foot:

> Ĭ sóme/ tĭmes thínk/ thăt név/ ĕr blóws/ sŏ réd/
>
> Thĕ Róse/ ăs whére/ sóme búr/ ĭed Cáe/ săr bléd;/
>
> Thăt év/ erў Hý/ ăcĭnth/ thĕ Gár/ dĕn wéars/
>
> Drópt ĭn/ hĕr láp/ frŏm sóme/ ónce lóve/ lў héad./

Although only the first line consists wholly of iambic feet, it is not hard to see that the prevailing or dominant foot of the stanza is iambic, and that the lines are based on a recurrent pattern of five feet. We thus designate the meter as iambic pentameter. Terms for other line lengths are:

one foot	monometer
two feet	dimeter
three feet	trimeter
four feet	tetrameter
six feet	hexameter
seven feet	heptameter
eight feet	octameter

A fuller description of the *Rubaiyat* stanza would indicate the rhyme scheme: *a a b a*. A handy way to notate both the rhyme scheme and the length of the line in feet is: *a a b a*^{5}.

The stanza from the *Rubaiyat* presents a very uncomplicated metrical situation. Some complexity begins to enter when we encounter lines like these, from Pope's "The Rape of the Lock":

Fávŏurs/tŏ nóne, ‖ tŏ áll/shĕ smíles/ĕxténds;/

Óft shĕ/rĕjécts, ‖ bŭt név/ĕr ónce/ŏffénds./

Here we come upon a strong, rhetorically meaningful caesura, or extrametrical pause, within the lines. The caesura here, positioned after the fourth syllable, near the middle of the line, is called a medial caesura. If it should occur near the beginning of the line, it is called an initial caesura; if near the end of the line, terminal. Caesuras, which are often marked by punctuation, can be said to correspond to breath pauses between musical phrases; in verse, their slight interruption of the propulsive metrical pattern can provide a kind of expressive counterpoint or opposition as well as enforcing the rhetorical sense, as, in the Pope example, the caesura provides a metrical fulcrum for the rhetorical antitheses. Some lines have more than one caesura; some have none. Unless the slight unpunctuated pause after *lap* in the last line of the *Rubaiyat* stanza be considered a caesura, those four lines have none.

To become sensitive to the presence of caesuras in English poems is to move toward both a heightened awareness of literary history and a new receptiveness to the art of texture in all the poems one encounters. In classical, Romance, and Old English verse the caesura is used in a fairly predictable way. It is only with the development in English of the staple iambic pentameter line—that ubiquitous and apparently permanent vehicle—that varied and expressive caesura placement (as in Chaucer) begins to become a subtle prosodic device. While in Old English verse the invariable medial caesura had been used to separate each line into two half-lines and thus to assert the regularity of the structure, in Modern English the caesura is more often used as a device of variety which helps mitigate metrical rigors as it shifts from position to position in successive lines. In formal verse, whether classical, Romance, or Old English, the medial position of the caesura is generally predictable; in verse aspiring to a greater flexibility and informality, we cannot anticipate the position of the pauses, and here they serve quite a different function.

The predictable medial caesura occurs with great regularity in the accentual, alliterative poetry of Old English:

> Hige sceal þe heardra, || heorte þe cenre,
> Mod sceal þe mare, || þe ure maegen lytlaþ.
> ("The Battle of Maldon")

It is also extremely regular in the staple line of French epic and dramatic verse, the syllabic alexandrine:

> Trois fois cinquante jours || le général naufrage
> Dégasta l'univers; || et fin d'un tel ravage
> (Du Bartas, "La Première Semaine")

It appears as a formalizing device in English blank verse of the early Renaissance as the verse seems to strain to break away from memories of its Old English ancestry:

> O knights, O squires, || O gentle blouds yborne,
> You were not borne, || al onely for your selves:
> (Gascoigne, "The Steel Glass")

Likewise much English Augustan poetry exploits the medial caesura, but for quite special effects of antithetical wit and irony:

> See Sin in State, || majestically drunk;
> Proud as a Peeress, || prouder as a Punk;
> Chaste to her Husband, || frank to all beside,
> A teeming Mistress, || but a barren Bride.
> (Pope, "Moral Essay II")

In seventeenth-century blank verse, on the other hand, and especially in Milton's, the placement of the caesura is often extremely flexible and surprising:

> Thus with the Year
> Seasons return, but not to me returns
> Day, || or the sweet approach of Ev'n or Morn.

> * * *

> And Bush with frizl'd hair implicit: || last
> Rose as in dance the stately Trees. . . .
> (*Paradise Lost*)

It is also deployed with flexibility in much modern iambic penta-meter verse:

> An aged man is but a paltry thing,
> A tattered coat upon a stick, || unless
> Soul clap its hands and sing, and louder sing
> For every tatter in its mortal dress. . . .
>   (Yeats, "Sailing to Byzantium")

From these examples it is clear that the caesura can be used in two quite antithetical ways: (1) as a device for emphasizing the formality of the poetic construction and for insisting on its dis-tance from colloquial utterance; and (2) as a device for investing fairly strict meters with something of the informal movement—the unpredictable pauses and hesitations—of ordinary speech. If the caesura occurs regularly in the medial position, we are dealing with a different kind of verse from that in which caesura place-ment is varied and unpredictable: which is to say that the whole metrical contract between poet and reader becomes a different one. Consider, for example, Frost's "Out, Out——"; here the caesuras are prevailingly medial and astonishingly unvaried:

> No one believed. || They listened at his heart.
> Little—less—nothing! || —and that ended it.
> No more to build on there. || And they, since they
> Were not the one dead, || turned to their affairs.

What Frost suggests by this reminiscence of formal caesura prac-tice is that a domestic rural disaster is being raised to the ele-vation of extremely formal art. We can contrast, on the other hand, the practice of T. S. Eliot in "Journey of the Magi." Here the caesuras are unexpectedly varied:

> There were times we regretted
> The summer palaces on slopes, || the terraces
>
>   *   *   *
>
> All this was a long time ago, || I remember,
> And I would do it again, || but set down
> This set down
> This: || were we led all that way for
> Birth or Death? . . .

Eliot, proceeding in an opposite direction from Frost, is lending
a colloquial air to a rhetoric which otherwise might seem excessively chill, distant, and unbelievable. Such are the expressive
potentialities for either formality or informality in the use of
caesuras either medially or with greater variation.

There is another complication to be aware of in scanning English lines. We must exercise a historical consciousness in pro-
nouncing sounds if we are to recover and relive the original
schemes of versification. And if we are concerned with accurate
and critically meaningful scansion, we must become skeptical of
"modernized" texts; otherwise we run the risk of modernizing—
and thus distorting—the original versification. For example: in
accentual-syllabic poetry with strong ambitions toward the formal
and the oratorical, poetic contractions or elisions are used to
keep contiguous lines equal in number of syllables. Although the
technical terms for various kinds of contractions are not essential,
it is useful to know them. We distinguish two basic kinds of contractions, synaeresis (sometimes called synaloepha) and syncope.
When contracting a word by synaeresis, the poet joins two vowels
to create a single syllable, a sort of nonce diphthong:

> Of man's first disobedience, and the fruit
> (*Paradise Lost*)

Here the *ie* in *disobedience* changes to what is called a *y*-glide,
and the word becomes *disobed-yence*. Its normal five syllables
are reduced to four to keep the line decasyllabic. Syncope, on the
other hand, is what we call either the omission of a consonant (as
in "ne'er") or the dropping of an unstressed vowel which is
flanked by consonants:

> Ill fares the land, to hastening ills a prey
> (Goldsmith, "The Deserted Village")

In this line *hastening,* normally trisyllabic, is reduced by syncope
to a dissyllable, and the line is thus kept within its decasyllabic
confines.

Poetic contractions like these are found most often in English
verse composed from the Restoration to the end of the eighteenth
century. In poetry of this period the contractions are often indi-

cated typographically by apostrophes: e.g., *hast'ning*. But in scanning we must observe the contractions whether indicated typographically or not, for the aesthetic of Augustan poetry assumes that each line will be regular in number of syllables, and this regularity is an indispensable part of what the lines are transmitting. Because the neglect or modernizing of such contractions distorts what these poems "say," the contractions must be heeded by the modern reader who wants to recreate for his own ear the genuine tone of a historical versification.

So far we have been considering mostly the rhythmical patterns manifested by the "prose sense" of the words in poetic lines, and until we master the art of understanding and marking the rhetorical emphasis of the words *as if they were prose* we are unprepared to venture upon the next step in scansion, a step fraught with the danger of *a priori* proceedings. This step involves allowing our scansions to reveal, *where appropriate,* the force of the abstract metrical pattern which presumably lies behind the actual rhythms of the words. As Joseph Malof has said, "One kind of energy in poetic language comes from the wrestling of abstract patterns with actual prose rhythms. The result is a compromise recorded in the scansion, which must therefore be sensitive to both opposing forces. Scansion should indicate, as far as possible, both the degree to which the natural prose rhythms are modified by the metrical law, and the degree to which the metrical law is forced to become amended by those elements in the prose rhythm that will not yield." What Mr. Malof is saying is that, once the metrical contract has been agreed to by both parties, an underlying "silent" metrical continuum proceeds through the poem, and that this abstract pattern, which the actual words are continuously either reinforcing or departing from, has the power now and then to force a metrical rather than a natural pronunciation of a word or phrase.

Consider what happens in these two lines of the old ballad of "Sir Patrick Spens"; the rising rhythm is so powerfully enforced in the early part of the first line that we are naturally invited to mispronounce the word *master* in order to let the purely metrical element have its way:

> And I fear, I fear, my dear master,
> That we will come to harm.

Another example: unless we are in the army, we generally pronounce the word *detail* with the accent on the second syllable.
That, at least, is the pronunciation prescribed in most dictionaries. Now if poetic rhythm were always supplied entirely by the
rhetorical emphasis of the actual words in their prose sense, and
never by the silent, continuing metrical background, the word
detail in the opening lines of Frost's "Directive" would invite its
normal prose pronunciation. But we find that it does not:

> Back out of all this now too much for us,
> Back in a time made simple by the loss
> Of detail, burned, dissolved, and broken off . . .

Here it is the meter itself that, regardless of the way we normally
pronounce the word, forces us on this occasion to pronounce it as
the poem demands we should.

At least two kinds of temptation toward mis-scansion offer
themselves when we permit a scansion to register the metrical as
well as the actual rhythm: there is first the general difficulty of
knowing what the dominant meter of a line is and the temptation
to simplify matters by mechanically reading some presumed
meter into the words before us; and secondly there is the difficulty
of mastering historical pronunciation and thus recovering the
rhythm actually implicit in the line regarded as a historical artifact. It is safe to say that only very infrequently will a metrical
pattern predominate so powerfully over the actual rhythm of the
language in a line that it will force the pronunciation to bend to
its will. If we must give a preference to either the metrical or the
actual, it is probably safest to err in scansion on behalf of the
actual rhythm. Proceeding *a priori* is as dangerous in prosody as
elsewhere.

What, finally, is scansion for? To scan only to conclude that a
poem is "written in iambic pentameter" is to do nothing significant. It is only as a basis for critical perception and ultimately for
critical judgment that scansion can justify itself. The sort of perception that scansion makes possible by translating sound into
visual terms can be illustrated in the *Rubaiyat* stanza with which
we began. Consider what happens in the last two lines of that
stanza:

Thăt év/erў Hý/ăcĭnth/thĕ Gár/dĕn wéars/

Drópt ĭn/hĕr lăp/frŏm sóme/ónce lóve/lў héad./

By giving us a clear visual representation of the metrical status of the words, the scansion of these two lines makes apparent the substitution of a trochee for the expected iamb at the beginning of the last line. This variation, which reinforces the shocking suddenness and rapidity of the fall of the drops of blood, constitutes a moment of high, although perhaps not the highest, technical accomplishment. It is to learn to appraise such accomplishments accurately that we scan at all.

3

Metrical Variations

Meter probably began as a mere mnemonic device, a way of helping bards and scholars memorize their epics and annals and genealogies, their medical prescriptions, legal codes, and recipes, before the days of printed books. When meter is used mnemonically it is essential that it be as regular as possible. The principle of expressive variation from a metrical norm is thus a relatively late metrical development. It is certainly the primary source of metrical pleasure for the modern critical reader. As Robert Frost puts it, "We enjoy the straight crookedness of a good walking stick."

We can discriminate three degrees of metrical competence in poets. In the lowest degree, exemplified by the effusions which appear in rural newspapers, we feel a metrical imperative either not at all or only very rarely:

I KISSED PA TWICE AFTER HIS DEATH
By Mattie J. Peterson

I kissed dear Pa at the grave,
  Then soon he was buried away;
Wreaths were put on his tomb,
  Whose beauty soon decay.

I lay down and slept after the burial;—
   I had started to school, I dreamed,
But had left my books at home,
   Pa brought them it seemed.

I saw him coming stepping high,
   Which was of his walk the way;
I had stopped at a house near by—
   His face was pale as clay.

When he lay under a white sheet
   On the morning after his decease,
I kissed his sad and sunken cheek,
   And hoped his spirit had found peace.

When he was having convulsions
   He feared he would hurt me;
Therefore told me to go away.
   He had dug artichokes for me.

Pa dug artichokes on that day,
   He never will dig anymore;
He has only paid the debt we owe.
   We should try to reach the shining shore.

Here so much effort is going into finding rhymes that little energy is left over for the meter.

In the middle range of metrical competence we find poems which establish in the first line a rigorously regular metric and then adhere religiously to it with little or no variation. Sackville and Norton's *Gorboduc* (1565), composed in an excessively regular blank verse, is such a work. Swinburne said of it: "Verse assuredly it is not; there can be no verse, where there is no modulation." The works of folk-poets like Edgar Guest and Henry Van Dyke belong to this second category. Their metrical regularity makes them remarkably easy to memorize and recite, and perhaps public recitation is what they are designed for:

I know that Europe's wonderful, yet something seems to lack:
The Past is too much with her, and the people looking back.
But the glory of the Present is to make the Future free—
We love our land for what she is and what she is to be.
                      (Henry Van Dyke, "America for Me")

The very regularity of the meter, indeed, is conceived to con-stitute a large part of the merit of such compositions.

In poems of the third and most sophisticated metrical kind, the entire function of meter is very different from what it is in poems of the second sort. Emerson's remark helps suggest the all-important difference: "It is not meters, but a meter-making argu-ment that makes a poem." Or as Pound puts it, "[Meter] can't be merely a careless dash off, with no grip and no real hold to the words and sense." In this kind of poem the poet establishes regularity only to depart from it expressively. When he does compose a metrically regular line it is not because the metrical scheme tells him to, but because something in the matter he is embodying impels him toward a momentary regularity. It is only with poems of this third metrical level that we shall be con-cerned: here we shall see meter used less as a mere ordering element than as an expressive one.

"Most arts," writes Pound, "attain their effect by using a fixed element and a variable." The fixed element in poetry is the received or contrived grid or framework of metrical regularity; the variable is the action of the rhythm of the language as it departs from this framework. This opposition between the "silent" or abstract metrical pattern and the actual language rhythm has been described by many terms which mean roughly the same thing: counterpoint, modulation, tension, syncopation, interplay, variation. It is probably true, as W. K. Wimsatt and Monroe Beardsley suggest, that "there is no line so regular (so *evenly* alternating weak and strong) that it does not show some tension. It is practically impossible to write an English line that will not in some way buck against the meter. Insofar as the line does approximate the condition of complete submission, it is most likely a tame line, a weak line." Tameness and weakness, for all the fraudulent pretense of vigor and manliness, are the metri-cal curse, ultimately, of lines like Van Dyke's, lines that are too regular or are regular for only extrinsic or mechanical reasons.

It almost goes without saying that the most expressive metrical variations are possible only in verse conceived in a tradition of more or less regular base rhythm. Variations of the kind we shall be considering are the province of a very specific and limited kind of poetry—namely, accentual-syllabic verse (or accentual verse with a high degree of syllabic regularity) written since the stabilization of Modern English early in the Renaissance. If English prosodic history has one great tradition, this is where we must go to find it.

If we are more or less traditional graphic scansionists, we will probably use the term *substitution* as the readiest way to describe metrical variations. Once a metrical pattern has been implied in a poem, we can say that variations in the rhythm occur through the introduction of substitute feet which here and there replace certain of the base feet. Such a way of talking is not likely to lead us astray so long as we remember that we are speaking in metaphors. In Yeats's lines that follow, for example, we can say that each contains a substitution for one of the expected iambic feet:

> Ăn ág/ĕd mán/ĭs bŭt/ă pál/trў thíng,/
>
> Ă tát/terĕd cóat/ŭpŏn/ă stíck,/ŭnléss/
>
> Sóul cláp/ĭts hánds/ănd síng,/ănd lóud/ĕr síng/
>
> Fŏr év/erў tát/tĕr ĭn/ĭts mór/tăl dréss/. . . .

Line 1 has a pyrrhic in the third position; line 2 a pyrrhic in the third; line 3 a spondaic (or perhaps trochaic) substitution in the first position; and line 4 a pyrrhic in the third. Here the substitutions serve both to relieve the metrical monotony of the long-continued, unvaried iambic pentameter and to allow the rhythmical structure to "give" and shape itself according to the rhetorical pressures of the statement. And the rhythmical shaping is noticeable only because it takes place against the background of the "silent" metrical continuum.

In the following lines from Arnold's "Dover Beach" we find substitutions used very specifically on behalf of the physical and emotional reinforcement of the sense:

> Lístĕn!/yŏu héar/thĕ grá/tĭng róar/
>
> Ŏf péb/blĕs whĭch/thĕ wáves/dráw báck,/ănd flíng,/
>
> Ăt thĕir/rĕtúrn,/ŭp thĕ/hígh stránd,/
>
> Bĕgín,/ănd céase,/ănd thén/ăgaín/bĕgín/. . . .

Against the established iambic background which precedes, the initial trochaic substitution in line I constitutes an unexpected reversal of rhythmical movement which emphasizes the new intensification in the speaker's address to his listener. To replace the trochee *Listen!* with an iamb like *But hark!* is to appreciate the power of the reversed initial foot to grab the reader. In line 2 the spondaic substitution in the fourth position implies and enacts the slowness of the seawave as it withdraws back upon itself, gathering force by accumulation like a coil spring to shoot itself up the beach. The pyrrhic substitution in the first position in line 3 is the rhythmical equivalent of the speed with which the wave flings itself up the sloping sands. And in line 4 the return to the regularity of unvaried iambic meter after these suggestive variations emphasizes rhythmically in this context the infinite, monotonous continuance of the waves' old kinetic process.

In addition to the strictly dissyllabic substitutions we have been considering, lines can also be varied by the addition or subtraction of unaccented syllables: these variations are accomplished, we can say, by trisyllabic or monosyllabic substitution. In duple measures the substitution of a trisyllabic foot for a dissyllabic one is a bolder practice than any we have seen so far, for it increases the syllabic length of the line and thus effaces one of the norms of predictability. Consider Yeats's variations here:

> Ónce óut/ŏf ná/tŭre Ĭ/ shăll né/vĕr táke/
>
> Mў bó/dĭlў fórm/frŏm á/nў ńa/tŭrăl thíng,/ . . .
> ("Sailing to Byzantium")

In the second and fifth positions of line 2 we find anapests replacing iambs, and the two trisyllabic substitutions swell the line to twelve instead of ten syllables, a weighty equivalent of the climactic revelation the line embodies. Even more venturesome is Frost's metrical practice at the beginning of his lyric "Come In," where, after establishing an initial rhythm very like anapestic trimeter in a poem which will prove to be prevailingly iambic, Frost reverses completely to a dactylic movement, and then presents a caesura and a monosyllable as the equivalent of a complete foot:

> Ăs Ĭ cáme/tŏ thĕ édge/ŏf thĕ wóods,/
>
> Thrúsh mŭsĭc ‖ —hárk!/

As we can deduce from these examples, the principles of expression through metrical variation are the following:

1. A succession of stressed syllables without the expected intervening unstressed syllables can reinforce effects of slowness, weight, or difficulty;
2. A succession of unstressed syllables without the expected intervening stressed syllables can reinforce effects of rapidity, lightness, or ease;
3. An unanticipated reversal in the rhythm (as in line 1 of the Arnold passage, or line 2 of the Frost) implies a sudden movement, often of discovery or illumination; or a new direction of thought, a new tone of voice, or a change or intensification of poetic address.

Before we consider some triumphant moments in English poetry of each of these principles, it might be well to make a cautionary point. We should understand clearly that although metrical variations can be displayed by scansion and analyzed dispassionately, when the poet performs them they are largely instinctual, a technique of his art so unconsciously mastered that he seldom pauses formally to debate a metrical alternative. Indeed, many poets whose work can be analyzed metrically according to the traditional foot system would undoubtedly be astonished to hear that they have indulged in anything like "substitution." The poet often composes according to the rhythms which his utterance supplies, and although these rhythms frequently turn out to consist of "base" and "substitute" feet, they do not necessarily begin that way.

At the same time, we may suspect that Alexander Pope, a highly self-conscious metrist, is one poet who is quite deliberately weighing and measuring feet in his famous passage from "An Essay on Criticism" designed to illustrate the first of our principles, the reinforcement of effects of weight or difficulty by the device of spondaic substitution:

> Whĕn Á/jăx stríves/sŏme róck's/vást wéight/tŏ thrów,/
>
> Thĕ líne/tóo lá/bŏurs, ănd/thĕ wórds/móve slów;/

Although a large part of the reinforcement is rhythmical here— the result of the spondaic substitution in the fourth position of line 1 and in the second and fifth positions of line 2—we should notice too the contribution of cacophony (that is, the effect of strain or difficulty resulting from the collocation of consonants difficult to pronounce rapidly). The conjunction of *s* sounds which prevents a normal, smooth transition from the pronunciation of one word to another and which enforces distinct and uncomfortable pauses (Aja*x* *s*trive*s* *s*ome) adds its own illusion of labor and difficulty. Whatever the exact contributions we assign to the metrical variations and the cacophony, there is no doubt that we feel as if physically exhausted when we have read this couplet. It makes us one with Ajax.

Throughout his career Pope seemed to treasure the device of spondaic substitution as one of the most effective techniques in his rhythmic repertory. In "Eloisa to Abelard" the intolerable tedium of the emasculated Abelard's future sexless years is implied by a crucial spondaic substitution. As Eloisa tells him:

> For thee the fates, severely kind, ordain
> A cool suspense from pleasure and from pain;
> Thў lífe/ă lóng/déad cálm/ŏf fíxed/rĕpóse;/
> No pulse that riots, and no blood that glows.

In "The Rape of the Lock" the "vast weight" of Lord Petre's favorite inert books—the mock-epic corollary of Ajax's vast rock —is suggested by a spondee:

> . . . ere Phoebus rose, he had implored
> Propitious heaven, and every power adored,
> But chiefly Love—to Love an Altar built
> Of twelve/vást Frénch/Romances, neatly gilt.

And later in the same poem the wise Clarissa is made to imply the weight and interminable weariness of old age by a judicious spondee:

> O! if to dance all night, and dress all day
> Charmed the small-pox, or chased/óld-áge/away;
> Who would not scorn what housewife's cares produce,
> Or who would learn one earthly thing of use?

In the "Essay on Man" a similar substitution—of two spondees this time—emphasizes rhythmically the apparent slowness of death's approach in old age:

> To each unthinking being, Heaven, a friend,
> Gives not the useless knowledge of its end:
> To Man imparts it; but with such a view
> As, while he dreads it, makes him hope it too:
> The hour concealed, and so remote the fear,
> Déath stíll/dráws néar/eř, né/věr séem/ǐng néar./

The recovery of iambic regularity in the final three feet of this last line constitutes an exquisite return to the optimistic normalities after a short sojourn, which proves to be largely a metrical one, among hints of the cheerless and the irrevocable. Pope's practice suggests that metrical variations exert their most memorable effects in very serious contexts—places where the most interesting mysteries of life and death are being plumbed. It is the very tiniest variation from the norm in these places that has power to wrench the heart, to persuade us that we are in the presence of superb physical as well as intellectual and moral wisdom.

But Pope is not so solemn a poet that he cannot enlist the same technique for merrier purposes. Here he is satirizing "heroes"—of the sort accepted as such in the context of "greatness" promulgated by Sir Robert Walpole—by exhibiting them to us in slow, spondaic motion:

> No less alike the Politic and Wise;
> All sly/slów thíngs,/with circumspective eyes:
> ("Essay on Man")

And the agony of effort in the following is almost physically unendurable: Timon, the *nouveau riche* who has built a grandiloquent villa, welcomes us to his heavy pile:

> My Lord advances with majestic mien,
> Smit with the mighty pleasure, to be seen:
> But soft,—with regular approach,—not yet,—
> First through the length of yon/hót tér/race sweat;

> And when up ten/stéep slópes/you've dragged your thighs,
> Just at his Study-door he'll bless your eyes.

In a similar way Ambrose Philips's literary constipation is rendered in the "Epistle to Arbuthnot" through double spondaic substitution:

> Just writes to make his barrenness appear,
> And strains from hard-/bóund bráins,/éight línes/a year.

And the assonance which links *strains, brains,* and *eight* associates the three words rhetorically as well as prosodically. Philips becomes the satiric victim of metrical variations again in the *Dunciad,* where, together with Nahum Tate, he is taxed by spondees with torpor. The Goddess of Dulness, we are told,

> . . . saw/slów Phíl/ips creep like Tate's/póor páge.

And it is largely through spondaic substitution that boredom, the prevailing atmosphere of the *Dunciad* world, is projected:

> Then mount the Clerks, and in one lazy tone
> Through the/lóng, héa/vy, painful page/dráwl ón./

Likewise the famous Universal Yawn demands a spondaic rendering:

> Lost was the Nation's Sense, nor could be found,
> While the/lóng, sól/emn Unison went round.

But brilliant as he is at managing the spondaic variation in iambic contexts, Pope is not unique: he takes his place in a long line of conventional metrists who have exploited this device to reinforce effects of weight or difficulty or slowness. The only thing mysterious about the device, actually, is the way it seldom fails to delight the reader. To trace some of its uses from the mid-sixteenth century to our own time is to develop a conviction of the essential technical unity of post-Renaissance English verse.

In 1559 Thomas Sackville, in the "Induction" to the *Mirror for Magistrates,* deploys the spondee to reinforce effects of size: the domain of Pluto is described as

> The wide/wáste plác/es and the hugy plain.

The technique of Pope's literary yawns and *longueurs* is foreshadowed by Edmund, in *King Lear,* who describes with the aid of spondees the tedium which may attend the marriage bed of the respectable; bastards, he says,

> . . . in the lusty stealth of nature, take
> More composition and fierce quality
> Than doth, within a/dúll, stále,/tíred béd,/
> Go to th'creating a whole tribe of fops. . . .

Time can be stretched by spondees, as both Ben Jonson and Andrew Marvell are aware. Condemning empty wits and fools in "An Epistle Answering to One that Asked To Be Sealed of the Tribe of Ben," Jonson declares:

> I have no portion of them, nor their deal
> Of news they get to strew out the/lóng méal./

And Marvell arranges spondees for a similar end in "To His Coy Mistress":

> Had we but world enough, and time,
> This coyness, lady, were no crime.
> We would sit down and think which way
> To walk, and pass our long/lóve's dáy./

In *Paradise Lost* the rebel angels who explore the infernal regions are put through a round of spondaic exercises which imply as much strength as Pope's Ajax is going to need a few years later:

> . . . through many a dark and dreary Vale
> They pass'd, and many a Region dolorous,
> O'er many a Frozen, many a Fiery Alp,
> Rócks, Cáves,/Lákes, Féns,/Bógs, Déns,/and shades of death.

And it seems typical of Milton's practice in spondaic substitution
to return to a very pronounced iambic regularity to re-establish
the metrical norm after these excursions into spondaic difficulty
and strain. For example:

> So eagerly the Fiend
> O'er bog or steep, through strait,/róugh, dénse,/or rare,
> With head,/hánds, wíngs,/or feet pursues his way,
> And swims or sinks, or wades, or creeps, or flies.

The technique of expressive spondaic substitution is handed
on to Thomas Gray, who uses spondees to reinforce a feeling
of the inert and the inorganic in the "Elegy":

> Can storied Urn or animated Bust
>   Back to its Mansion call the fleeting Breath?
> Can Honour's Voice provoke the silent Dust,
>   Or Flatt'ry sooth the dull/cóld Eár/of Death?

And in the same poem spondaic substitution is enlisted to
lengthen the lingering backward look which the dying cast on
the "warm precincts" of their lives:

> For who, to dumb Forgetfulness a prey,
>   This pleasing anxious Being e'er resign'd,
> Left the warm Precincts of the cheerful Day,
>   Nor cast/óne lóng/ing, ling'ring Look behind?

George Crabbe, as if mindful of the use of spondees by Ben
Jonson and Pope for purposes of satire, exposure, and correction,
exploits the tradition in "The Village" to embody the weariness
of the country laborers' day:

> Or will you deem them amply paid in health,
> Labour's fair child, that languishes with wealth?
> Go then! and see them rising with the sun,
> Through a/lóng cóurse/of daily toil to run.

And suggestions of the inert and the laborious attach to the
famous spondee in Wordsworth's "A Slumber Did My Spirit

Seal." Here Wordsworth, like Milton, seems careful to return
to the strictest kind of iambic regularity after the substitution, as
if to throw the spondee into even bolder relief:

> No motion has she now, no force,
> She neither hears nor sees;
> Rólled róund/in earth's diurnal course,
> Wĭth rócks,/ănd stónes,/ănd trées./

While most poets like to introduce spondaic substitutions
initially or medially, Keats seems fond of introducing them at
the ends of lines; indeed, terminal substitution is a hallmark of
the Keatsian style. Here he addresses the Grecian urn, which, like
Gray's "storied urn," lives in a world where time is slowed to
eternity:

> Thou still unravish'd bride of quietness,
> Thou foster-child of silence and/slów tíme./

The end of the line attracts the Keatsian spondee also in "Ode
to a Nightingale," where the crucial line is slowed almost to a
total stop by the spondee which rounds off the image of cessation:

> Now more than ever seems it rich to die,
> To cease upon the midnight with/nó paín./

And the plethora of terminal spondees in "La Belle Dame sans
Merci" seems to fix the situation of that poem in a world where
time has quite stopped:

> I saw their starv'd lips in the gloom
> With horrid warning gaped wide,
> And I awoke, and found me here
> On the cold/híll síde./
> And this is why I sojourn here
> Alone and palely loitering,
> Though the sedge is wither'd from the lake,
> And no/bírds síng./

One of Wilfred Owen's favorite predecessors was Keats, as we might infer from the way Owen revises a line in his sonnet "Anthem for Doomed Youth," written in 1917 to memorialize the passive young victims of the Great War. Their deaths will be noted, Owen writes, not by conventional religious exequies but by

> The shrill demented choirs of wailing shells,
> And bugles calling sad across the shires.

But the regularity of that last line seems too "normal" if not jaunty for an occasion redolent of cessation and arrested time, and Owen revises it to read:

> And bugles calling for them from/sád shíres./

Compared with Keats, and even with Owen, Tennyson uses spondaic substitution in "Ulysses" in a more facile and obvious way:

> The lights begin to twinkle from the rocks;
> The long/dáy wánes;/the slow/móon clímbs;/thĕ déep/
> Móans róund/with many voices. . . .

This is showy but easy. We get the feeling that one substitution in line 2 would be quite enough: two is too many, and the third, which calls excessive attention to the speaker's technical powers, almost negates the skill of the first. Tennyson has more success in "In Memoriam," where he is content to leave well enough alone:

> Yet in these ears, till hearing dies,
> One set/slów béll/will seem to toll
> The passing of the sweetest soul
> That ever look'd with human eyes.

The fullness and heaviness of excessively saddened or of excessively joyous hearts is one constant in English poetry which seems to invite a spondaic rendering. Here is Tennyson in "The Princess":

> I would you had her, Prince, with all my heart,
> With my/fúll héart:/

And then there is Hardy's "Darkling Thrush," a bird which can be regarded both as a thematic and a prosodic ancestor of Frost's thrush in "Come In." Like Frost's thrush, Hardy's makes its appearance in the midst of a startling trochaic reversal in line 2; and the heart's fullness naturally takes a spondaic rhythm in line 3:

> At once a voice arose among
> Thĕ bléak/twígs ŏv/ĕrhéad/
> Ĭn ă/fúll-héart/ĕd év/ĕnsŏng/
> Of joy illimited.

But lest we forget that spondaic substitution is as rich an effect in comic as in serious contexts, we should recall the vast dimensions of Fra Lippo Lippi's belly: what he appreciates in monastic life, he tells us, is

> the good bellyful,
> The warm serge and/thĕ rópe/thăt góes/áll róund,/
> And day-long blessed idleness beside!

And a different kind of spondaic comedy, the result of a focus on heaviness rather than on sheer size, attends the remark of the speaker in Eliot's "Portrait of a Lady":

> Mў smíle/fálls héav/ĭlў/among the bric-à-brac.

Ever since the Renaissance, English poets have delighted to suggest the presumably slowed circulation of chilled, thickened, or perhaps even "tired" blood by recourse to spondaic substitution. Thus Juliet in the fourth act, suspecting trouble ahead, says:

> Ĭ háve/ă fáint/cóld féar/thrílls thrŏugh/mў véins./

And the Ghost addressing Hamlet reverses his rhythm entirely with a trochee before invoking the customary "chilled blood" spondee:

> I could a tale unfold whose lightest word
> Would harrow up thy soul,/fréeze thў/yóung blóod,/
> Make thy two eyes, like stars, start from their spheres.

In "The Rime of the Ancient Mariner" Coleridge executes a virtuoso performance in the same effect:

> Her lips were red, her looks were free,
> Her locks were yellow as gold:
> Her skin was white as leprosy,
> The Nightmare Life-in-Death was she,
> Whŏ thícks/mán's blóod/wĭth cóld./

Tennyson does the same in "In Memoriam," even though he conceives of human anatomy more in terms of industrial machinery than perhaps his total imagery warrants:

> Be near me when my light is low,
> Whĕn thĕ/blóod créeps,/and the nerves prick
> And tingle; and the heart is sick,
> And all the wheels of Being slow.

Although almost any unexpected substitution can be used to signal surprise, to illuminate a sudden alteration in idea or emotion, or to mark a hiatus or interruption, the spondee is a favorite foot for this purpose. Frequently it is used in juxtaposition with a pyrrhic, which serves to prepare for the spondee as if by depriving us of a stress and thus making us desire two in succession all the more. Gavin Ewart, in a poem about listening to phonograph records titled "78's," does it this way:

> The house is now pulled down.
> I know exactly where the scratches come
> In jazz that moves me like the poetry
> Of Pasolini (I have 'grown up' too) .
>
> And later, in my teens, I knew (and know)
> Whĕre thĕ/ŭnnát/ŭrăl/breáks cáme/ĭn thĕ sým/phŏnĭes.
> Beginning with Beethoven I worked my way up
> At 78 (and 80) revolutions per minute.

One way of describing the metrical situation of line 6 here would
be to call the line an iambic-based hexameter with only one
iambic foot (the second), and with bold pyrrhic substitution in
the first, third, and sixth positions. Whichever way we decide
to mark or count the feet, however, we can hardly miss the
significant adaptation of rhythm to meaning, in which the clause
"the unnatural breaks came," with its pyrrhic and spondee,
interrupts the rhythmic continuum of the line just as the breaks
themselves once interrupted the continuum of the recorded
symphonies.

One of Pope's wittiest metrical exhibitions occurs in the
"Essay on Criticism" where the joint force of the two equally
stressed syllables of a spondee is made to underlie and support
the "joint force" of the elements of physical beauty:

> 'Tis not a lip or eye we beauty call,
> Bŭt thĕ/jóint fórce,/and full result of all.

The same kind of sudden physical force is given a spondaic
embodiment when Pope speaks of critics who admire bright
ideas and clever images in poems at the expense of all other
elements:

> Some to *Conceit* alone their taste confine,
> Ănd glítt/'rĭng thóughts/strúck oút/ăt év/erў líne./

This resembles Chatterton's reliance on spondaic and trochaic
substitution to introduce action suddenly in his song of the
"Thyrde Mynstrelle" from *Aella;* even Chatterton's pseudo-
medieval diction and spelling cannot disguise his happy participation in a postmedieval metrical tradition:

> Whanne Autumpne blake and sonne-brente doe appere,
> Wĭth hўs/góulde hónde/gúyltĕynge/thĕ fáll/ĕynge léfe./
> [When Autumn naked and sunburnt does appear,
> With his gold hand gilding the falling leaf]

And Swift is also a master of the spondee as a corollary of
sudden physical action. In "Baucis and Philemon," after relating
the metamorphosis of the two elderly lovers into yew trees, Swift

introduces a crucial spondaic substitution which not only emphasizes the sudden physical vigor of the action but also serves to signal one of the poem's most conspicuous antiheroic deflations:

> Old Good-man *Dobson* of the Green
> Remembers he the Trees has seen;
> He'll talk of them from Noon till Night,
> And goes with Folks to shew the Sight: . . .
> Points out the Place of either *Yew;*
> Here *Baucis,* there *Philemon* grew.
> Till once, a Parson of our Town,
> Tŏ ménd/hĭs Bárn,/cút *Báu*/cĭs dówn./

This use of the spondee to reinforce the suddenness and force of a vigorous action is a treasured traditional effect in English poetry, as we can appreciate when we juxtapose, say, Marlowe's erotic stallion image in "Hero and Leander,"

> . . . nothing more than counsel lovers hate;
> For as a hot proud horse highly disdains
> To have his head controlled, but breaks the reins,
> Spíts fórth/the ringled bit, and with his hooves
> Checks the submissive ground, so that he loves,
> The more he is restrained, the worse he fares. . . .

with something like Pope's portrait of Lord Hervey in the "Epistle to Arbuthnot," where the wicked peer, envisaged very like Satan "Squát lĭke/ă tóad,/clóse ăt/thĕ éar/ŏf Éve,/" spits out not elements of harness but the nastier elements of himself:

> Whether in florid impotence he speaks,
> And, as the prompter breathes, the puppet squeaks;
> Or at the ear of *Eve,* familiar Toad,
> Hálf fróth,/hálf vé/nŏm, spíts/hĭmsélf/ăbróad./

The technique assists William Cowper:

> Obscurest night involved the sky,
> The Atlantic billows roared,

> When such a destined wretch as I
> Wáshed héad/long from on board.
> ("The Castaway")

For all his radical suspicion of traditional poetic devices, Blake has recourse to the same technique:

> And every sand becomes a gem
> Reflected in the beams divine;
> Blówn báck/they blind the mocking eye,
> But still in Israel's paths they shine.
> ("Mock On, Mock On, Voltaire, Rousseau")

Yeats uses it in "The Statues" as he describes the wonderful physical appeal of the anatomical proportions enunciated by Pythagoras:

> But boys and girls, pale from the imagined love
> Of solitary beds, knew what they were, . . .
> And pressed at midnight in some public place
> Líve líps/upon a plummet-measured face.

And something of the same effect of instinctive impulsiveness attaches to Frost's similar spondee in "Dust of Snow":

> The way a crow
> Shóok dówn/on me
> The dust of snow
> From a hemlock tree
>
> Has given my heart
> A change of mood
> And saved some part
> Of a day I had rued.

Less abundantly encountered is what can be regarded as the opposite effect—depending on the second of our general principles —namely, the reinforcement of illusions of rapidity, lightness, or ease by the use of the pyrrhic foot in substitution, or by any unexpected juxtaposition of unstressed syllables. The classic example is provided by Pope in the "Essay on Criticism"; the couplet follows directly the one in which Ajax is depicted striving to throw his rock's vast weight:

> Not so, when swift Camilla scours the plain,
> Flíes ŏ'er/th'ŭnbénd/ĭng córn,/ănd skíms/ălŏng/thĕ máin./

In his *Life of Pope,* Samuel Johnson, always skeptical of the claims of "representative meter," exulted to point out that the last line—a so-called alexandrine—is "by one time [i.e., foot] longer" than the line depicting Ajax's labors, and that it therefore must be incapable of transmitting prosodically an effect of lightness or speed. But Johnson seems to have missed the point. By making his "fast" pyrrhic-substitution line one foot longer than his "slow" spondaic-substitution line, Pope is showing off: he is deliberately making his job as hard as possible; he is performing the metrical equivalent of shouting, "Look! No hands!" The point, after all, is not what the line looks like metrically but rather what its effects on the reader actually are. The transmission of expressive rhythm to the reader is always the result of artistic illusion, and the effect that works, no matter how "impossible" or "illogical," is the only one to be valued. As I. A. Richards wisely says, "The notion that there is any virtue in regularity or variety, or in any other formal feature, apart from its effects upon us, must be discarded before any metrical problem can be understood." Thus the number of feet in Pope's alexandrine, together with the actual time consumed in its reading or recitation, is irrelevant: the important thing is the effect that—no matter how irrationally or illogically—the line transmits.

Pyrrhic substitution is used with great skill by Pope also in "Moral Essay IV" to produce an effect not only of levity but even of the fast triple-time of a jig. Timon's vulgar private chapel with its inappropriate devotional music is under inspection:

> And now the Chapel's silver bell you hear,
> That summons you to all the Pride of Prayer:
> Light quirks of Music, broken and uneven,
> Máke thĕ/sóul dánce/ŭpŏn/ă jíg/tŏ héa/vĕn./

The expansion of these last two lines from ten to eleven syllables is caused by the feminine rhyme, and we must scan the lines as if each contained, at the end, a supernumerary syllable. Such a scansion is appropriate for reasons of historical accuracy: in the eighteenth century the substitution of trisyllabic for dissyllabic feet is not good form, and our scansion of such poems should reflect as nearly as it can the metrical conceptions of the authors.

On the other hand, in scanning a similar passage in Browning's "Fra Lippo Lippi," written over a century later, it is appropriate for our scansion to indicate the substitutions as trisyllabic feet, for by the nineteenth century trisyllabic substitution had become a metrical convention. But no matter how we scan, no one can fail to delight in the following, where Browning exploits the principle that, in the context of alternating stressed and unstressed which constitutes the abstract framework of blank verse, the presentation of a sequence of unstressed syllables (even the sequence of two that comprises the first part of an anapestic foot) can convey an illusion of speed or lightness. Here Lippi is alluding to some young girls and indicating their effect on him:

> Scarce had they turned the corner when a titter
> Lĭke thĕ skíp/pĭng ŏf ráb/bĭts bў móon/lĭght—three slim shapes,
> And a face that looked up . . . zooks, sir, flesh and blood,
> That's all I'm made of.

Finally, trochaic substitution in iambic contexts is the customary metrical technique for producing the third of our general effects—the effect of sudden movement or of a surprising emphasis or of a change in direction or tone—although, as we have seen, any foot (even the spondee) which constitutes a distinct reversal of the prevailing metrical pattern will tend to convey the same effect. There are three general positions in the line where trochaic substitution occurs: in the first position, in the middle, and at the end. In the first position trochaic substitution is extremely common—indeed, this one variation is the most common in all English poetry. It is less common in medial positions. And it is very uncommon in the terminal position. Substitution in each position tends to transmit its own unique kind of effects.

In the first position trochaic substitution most often supports the force of active verbs whose effect is to surprise, to enlighten

suddenly, or even to horrify. The great classic repository of this
effect is *Paradise Lost,* whose initial trochees seem to have colored
the practice of all subsequent poets working in anything like
accentual-syllabic meter. Here in Book VI, Christ's forces are
depicted overcoming Satan's:

> Dróve thĕm/before him Thunder-struck, pursu'd
> With terrors and with furies to the bounds
> And Crystal wall of Heav'n, which op'ning wide,
> Róll'd ín/ward, and a spacious Gap disclos'd
> Into the wasteful Deep; the monstrous sight
> Stróok thĕm/with horror backward, but far worse
> Úrg'd thĕm/behind; headlong themselves they threw
> Dówn frŏm/the verge of Heav'n, Eternal wrath
> Búrnt áf/ter them to the bottomless pit.

Although the passage exhibits other expressive variations (consider the force of the reversal in *headlong,* line 7), the trochees
underlying the active verbs at the beginnings of lines are especially vigorous just because they occur initially: even in lines so
boldly run-on as these, an initial substitution has the effect of
occurring after a pause—the pause which the eye makes in moving
from the end of one line to the beginning of the next. Like a
sudden drum beat after silence, the trochaic syllable, when it
occurs initially, has the power almost to stun.

The effect is more tender but no less powerful here, in Book IX,
where, encouraged by Eve's bad example, Adam

> . . . scrupl'd not to eat
> Against his better knowledge, not deceiv'd,
> But fondly overcome with Female charm.
> Earth trembl'd from her entrails, as again
> In pangs, and Nature gave a second groan,
> Sky low'r'd, and muttering Thunder, some sad drops
> Wépt ăt/completing of the mortal Sin
> Original.

The spondee of *sad drops* is heavy and heart-rending enough,
but after the slight pause occasioned by the end of the preceding

line, *Wept at* projects itself toward us with almost unbearable power. The initial trochee here is enlisted on behalf of horror complicated by overtones of tenderness and sympathy.

An illusion of sheer physical power, on the other hand, is the effect of the initial trochee which reinforces the active verbs in Adam's speculations in Book X about the operations of lightning:

> Or by collision of two bodies grind
> The Air attrite to Fire, as late the Clouds
> Jústlĭng/or pusht with Winds rude in thir shock
> Tíne thĕ/slant Lightning, whose thwart flame driv'n down
> Kíndlĕs/the gummy bark of Fir or Pine.

And in "Lycidas," Milton deploys the same device to reinforce an illusion of sudden and even awkward motion:

> I com to pluck your Berries harsh and crude,
> And with forc'd fingers rude,
> Sháttĕr/your leaves before the mellowing year.

At the end of the same poem an illusion of a sudden and surprising glory is the fruit of this device:

> So sinks the day-star in the Ocean bed,
> And yet anon repairs his drooping head,
> And tricks his beams, and with new spangled Ore
> Flámes ĭn/the forehead of the morning sky.

As if tutored by Milton, the poets of succeeding centuries have treasured the device of initial trochaic substitution with active verbs for effects of sudden force or violence. Here is Pope in the "Epistle to Fortescue" lashing about him at folly and crime:

> What? arm'd for virtue when I point the pen,
> Bránd thĕ/bold front of shameless guilty men;
> Dásh thĕ/proud gamester in his gilded car;
> Báre thĕ/mean heart that lurks beneath a *Star*.

Edward Fitzgerald, in the *Rubaiyat,* suddenly pulls down a tent:

> 'Tis but a Tent where takes his one day's rest
> A Sultan to the Realm of Death addrest;
>   The Sultan rises, and the dark Ferrash
> Stríkes, ănd/prepares it for another Guest.

Matthew Arnold injects sudden horror into the threat of military alarms in "Dover Beach," even though his verb is passive:

> And we are here as on a darkling plain,
> Swépt wĭth/confused alarms of struggle and flight,
> Where ignorant armies clash by night.

Housman, in "Eight O'Clock," suddenly animates the clock in the town hall which is striking the signal for the hanging of the "lad":

> He stood, and heard the steeple
>   Sprínklĕ/the quarters on the morning town.

And in "The Chestnut Casts His Flambeaux" Housman enacts the merciless violence of an insensate nature:

> The chestnut casts his flambeaux, and the flowers
> Stréam frŏm/the hawthorn on the wind away,
> The doors clap to, the pane is blind with showers.
> Pass me the can, lad; there's an end of May.

The initial stress assists Emily Dickinson to project the precision and decisiveness with which the railway train stops in "I Like To See It Lap the Miles":

> . . . then a quarry pare
>
> To fit its sides, and crawl between,
> Complaining all the while
> In horrid, hooting stanza;
> Then chase itself down hill
>
> And neigh like Boanerges;
> Then, punctual as a star,

Stóp—docile and omnipotent—
At its own stable door.

Yeats, in "A Prayer for My Son," emphasizes the violent suddenness of the act of philistine reprisal he fears:

> . . . they know
> Of some most haughty deed or thought
> That waits upon his future days,
> And would through hatred of the bays
> Bríng thăt/to nought.

Eliot's Prufrock has apparently learned a fully expressive versification from something like Milton's "Shatter your leaves":

> I should have been a pair of ragged claws
> Scúttlĭng/across the floors of silent seas.

There is a more delicate but no less startling effect in the depiction in "The Waste Land" of the fate of Phlebas the Phoenician's bones:

> Phlebas the Phoenician, a fortnight dead,
> Forgot the cry of gulls, and the deep sea swell
> And the profit and loss.
> 　　　　　　　　A current under sea
> Pícked hĭs/bones in whispers. As he rose and fell
> He passed the stages of his age and youth
> Entering the whirlpool.

We can gauge the amazing force of the initial trochee which is made to coincide with an active verb by comparing one of Eliot's passages with the original to which it alludes. Goldsmith's

> When lovely woman stoops to folly,
> And finds too late that men betray

remains within the pleasantly predictable, manageable world of the iambic. But by merely introducing an initial trochee, Eliot introduces hints of the awful, especially when this substitution constitutes the sole appearance of a trochee in the stanza:

> When lovely woman stoops to folly, and
> Pácĕs/about her room again, alone,
> She smoothes her hair with automatic hand,
> And puts a record on the gramophone.

The effect is like that in "Sweeney Among the Nightingales":

> The silent man in mocha brown
> Spráwls ăt/the window-sill and gapes.

W. H. Auden is a superb metrist, and we are not surprised that he has fully mastered this device. Here he exploits it twice in succession in "In Memory of W. B. Yeats":

> Intellectual disgrace
> Stáres frŏm/every human face,
> And the seas of pity lie
> Lócked ănd/frozen in each eye.

And in "The Fall of Rome" he seems to recall the practice of Housman in "The Chestnut Casts His Flambeaux," where the rainy wind, animated angrily by an initial trochee, betrays as little sympathy with man's fate:

> The piers are pummelled by the waves;
> In a lonely field the rain
> Láshĕs/an abandoned train.

Finally, an awareness of the long technical tradition of initial stressing which coincides with an active verb helps us to perceive the technical orthodoxy of a poet sometimes taxed with heterodoxy. Consider the opening of line 2 of Dylan Thomas's "The Force that Through the Green Fuse Drives":

> The force that through the green fuse drives the flower
> Dríves mў/green age; . . .

But lines begin with many other things than verbs. When it is a modifier—an adverb or adjective—that is coinciding with an

initial trochee, we often get a strong reinforcement of an effect of
sudden quiet, as in Wordsworth's "It Is a Beauteous Evening":

> It is a beauteous evening, calm and free,
> The holy time is quiet as a Nun
> Bréathlĕss/with adoration;

or in Keats's "On First Looking into Chapman's Homer":

> . . . like stout Cortez when with eagle eyes
> He star'd at the Pacific—and all his men
> Look'd at each other with a wild surmise—
> Sílĕnt,/upon a peak in Darien.

Indeed, this last example happily exhibits the different effects
produced by the initial trochee when it coincides with different
syntactical elements. The initial verbal trochee of line 3 (*Look'd
at*) functions, like Milton's, to transmit an effect of sudden vigor;
but the initial modifying trochee of the last line works on us
inversely by transmitting an effect of sudden calm.

Substantives in an initial trochaic (or spondaic) situation seem
to evoke a slightly different response. An illusion of absolute
finality is often transmitted by a noun in an initial stressed position. Listen, for example, to Milton's lyric meditation at the
beginning of Book III of *Paradise Lost:*

> Thus with the Year
> Séasŏns/return, but not to me returns
> Dáy, ŏr/the sweet approach of Ev'n or Morn;

or to Marvell's findings in "To His Coy Mistress":

> But at my back I always hear
> Tíme's wíng/ed chariot hurrying near;

—and as if unsatisfied that he has urged his rhythmic revelation
sufficiently, Marvell undertakes it again in the next couplet:

> And yonder all before us lie
> Désĕrts/of vast eternity.

Robert Frost's tiny masterpiece "Nothing Gold Can Stay" uses initial substantive trochees to similar effect. In this poem we find only two initial trochees, and both coincide with nouns, one at the opening of the first line, one at the opening of the last. The two substantive trochees might be said to function as an envelope of certainty, a fixed container suggestive of certainty and finality. If we are sufficiently schooled in the conventions of metrical variations—if we recall what Milton and Marvell have done with this same effect—we are in an advantageous position to determine from its rhythmic usages the exact tone of the poem:

> Nătŭre's/ first green is gold,
> Her hardest hue to hold.
> Her early leaf's a flower;
> But only so an hour.
> Then leaf subsides to leaf.
> So Eden sank to grief,
> So dawn goes down to day.
> Nŏthĭng/ gold can stay.

Even folk and "unsophisticated" compositions do not disdain the device of the startling initial trochee, as in this graffito from a U.S. Army latrine:

> Soldiers who wish to be a hero
> Are practically zero.
> But those who wish to be civilians,
> Jésŭs,/ they run into millions.

In medial positions trochaic substitution is fairly frequent, although not as common as at the beginning of lines. It is often used like the medial spondee to reinforce images of sudden action, as in Book IV of *Paradise Lost,* where speaking jointly to their Maker, Adam and Eve comment on the heavy fecundity of Eden:

> . . . this delicious place
> For us too large, where thy abundance wants
> Părtá/kĕrs, ănd/ ŭncrópt/ fálls tŏ/ thĕ gróund./

A more violent action is the trochaic rearing of the bridled stallion in Marlowe; the horse practically stands up right out of the poem:

> For as a hot proud horse/híghlў̆/dĭsdaíns/
> To have his head controlled, but breaks the reins. . . .

In "The Tower" Yeats manipulates the device with his customary metrical brilliance:

> I pace upon the battlements and stare
> On the foundations of a house, or where
> Tree, like a sooty finger,/stárts frŏm/the earth.

The same device is useful for comic purposes, as Charles Cotton demonstrates in his delightful epigram on the drunkard:

> The drunkard now supinely snores,
> His load of ale/swéats thrŏugh/his pores;
> Yet when he wakes, the swine shall find
> A crapula remains behind.

If we replace line 2 here with something like

> His load of ale comes out his pores

we can sense how much energy that medial trochee alone supplies.

Trochees in the terminal position, on the other hand, are extremely rare. One of the reasons would seem to be the difficulty of reversing a generally rising metrical sequence after, usually, four successive occurrences of it. It is as if the more iambic feet one writes in succession, the greater will be the difficulty of reversing the rhythm except at the beginning or perhaps in the middle of a *new* line. Some of the very few successful terminal trochees we encounter are employed to transmit a sophisticated and slightly weary sardonic effect. Thus Donne in his "Third Satire":

> Kind pity chokes my spleen; brave scorn forbids
> Those tears to issue which swell my/éyelĭds./

Thus Pope, in the "Epistle to Arbuthnot," on the annotations of textual editors:

> Pretty! in amber to observe the forms
> Of hairs, or straws, or dirt, or grubs, or worms!
> The things, we know, are neither rich nor rare,
> But wonder how the devil they/gót thĕre./

And thus Ezra Pound in "Mauberley" on the distinction between admirable and reprehensible poetic careers:

> His true Penelope was Flaubert,
> He fished by obstinate isles;
> Observed the elegance of Circe's hair
> Rather than the mottoes on/sún-dĭals./

A similar tone of the sardonic attaches to Yeats's use of the terminal trochee in "Among School Children":

> Better to smile on all that smile, and show
> There is a comfortable kind of old/scárecrŏw./

And to Auden's disposition of the same device:

> I sit in one of the dives
> On Fifty-second Street
> Uncertain and afraid
> As the clever hopes expire
> Of a low dishonest/décăde./

All this accretion of irony and derision which attends the terminal trochee when it appears in a generally skeptical context can be exploited by a skillful contemporary metrist like Donald Hall; in "Christmas Eve at Whitneyville, 1955," addressing his father, he does so:

> Tonight you lie in Whitneyville again,
> Near where you lived, and near the woods or farms
> Which Eli Whitney settled with the men
> Who worked at mass-producing/fírĕarms./

But the terminal trochee has another use, and one wholly different from its function as a trigger of irony. In a different context it can be used to reinforce a tone of colloquial "sincerity," to persuade us momentarily that we are in the presence less of a poetic illusionist assembling an artifact than that of a simple, straightforward speaker whose open commitment to what he is saying is so uncomplicated by doubts or irony that it would be a distinct discourtesy not to take his words at face value. There is something in the literary ambitions of late eighteenth- and early nineteenth-century lyric that urges it toward the terminal trochee to reinforce its effects of simplicity and sincerity. We find a suggestion of the "sincere" terminal trochee in Chatterton's "Mynstrelles Songe" from *Aella,* where a female speaker, apparently mindful of Ophelia's fate, mourns her lover:

> Mie love ys dedde,
> Gon to hys/déath-bĕdde,/
> Al under the wyllowe tree.

It is perhaps from Chatterton's work that Keats first learned to manage the device. But wherever he went for his technical lessons, there is little doubt that he is the great English master of the terminal trochee, which he is fond of using in the very first lines of poems as if to establish at the outset of his apostrophic addresses a tone of absolutely breathless, but no less intelligent, ingenuousness. Consider, for example,

> Bright star, would I were steadfast as/thóu ařt!/

or the opening of "To Sleep":

> O soft embalmer of the still/mídnĭght./

The effect is that of a poetic sensibility so fully committed to its convictions that it easily overrides the mere academic and technical tradition of iambic endings in iambic lines. But it is important to perceive that, for all its bold air of departure from the conventional, Keats's practice is disciplined by his rigorous empirical sense: he knows what effect the terminal trochee will have on the reader, and in this way his metrical taste is informed by his knowledge that he and his reader hold certain metrical conventions in common, certain accustomed ways of responding to certain traditional symbolic stimuli.

Now that we have considered the most common sorts of metrical variations, we should look at the scheme of overstressing practiced by Gerard Manley Hopkins and termed "sprung rhythm." He distinguishes it from what he calls common or running rhythm, that is, accentual-syllabic or accentual rhythm in which accented syllables tend to alternate with unaccented ones. Hopkins wanted his poetry to be stronger than standard poetry or prose, and he conceived that strength resides in stress. He thus devised sprung rhythm to provide his poems with a majority of stressed syllables. As he says, "Why, if it is forcible in prose to say *lashed rod,* am I obliged to weaken this in verse, which ought to be stronger, not weaker . . . ?" Thus he posits that "even one stressed syllable may make a foot, and consequently two or more stresses may come running [i.e., adjoin each other], which in common rhythm can, regularly speaking, never happen." What he is implying is that the poet working in sprung rhythm composes almost as if the spondee were a base rather than a substitute foot. He can thus project effects of slowness and weight more effectively than in an "alternating" prosodic system where frequent unstressed syllables occur.

Hopkins points out that sprung rhythm is common in nursery rhymes. A good example is

> One, two,
> Buckle my shoe. . . .

where the first line is in sprung, the second in "running" rhythm. In

> March dust, April showers
> Bring forth May flowers. . . .

both lines can be considered sprung if *showers* and *flowers* are considered monosyllabic. Sprung rhythm is essentially a system of overstressing which accords the fullest possible recognition to the accentual character of the English language.

By approximating the movement of emotion-charged natural speech, sprung rhythm's effectiveness lies in projecting a tone of seriousness, frankness, and intimate emotional involvement. Like Keats's terminal trochees, it transmits an illusion of a total, if one-dimensional, commitment to the seriousness of the subject. Perhaps one weakness of sprung rhythm, however, is that it seems inappropriate to any other—and more complicated—tone. Comedy in it would seem unlikely, and wit all but impossible. Hopkins's "At the Wedding March" suggests the kind of materials and tone to which sprung rhythm seems best adapted (the stress markings are Hopkins's own) :

> God with honour hang your head,
> Groom, and grace you, bride, your bed
> With lissome scions, sweet scions,
> Out of hallowed bodies bred.
> Each be other's comfort kind:
> Déep, déeper than divined,
> Divine charity, dear charity,
> Fast you ever, fast bind.
>
> Then let the march tread our ears:
> I to him turn with tears
> Who to wedlock, his wonder wedlock,
> Déals tríumph and eternal years.

Tears and O's and Ah's and ecstatic wonder are Hopkins's staples, and it is in the service of these effects that sprung rhythm justifies itself. But the ultimate limitation of sprung rhythm seems to be indicated in Hopkins's own comment: "Sprung rhythm cannot be counterpointed." The system is a scheme of variations which has an insufficient framework to vary from. And after we have seen the abundant riches embodied in techniques of variation from stated and precise public norms, we may be skeptical of the varied expressive possibility of prosodic systems which cannot be counterpointed.

4

The Historical Dimension

Before we can proceed to our main business with meter, namely the use of metrical analysis as a tool of critical judgment, we must explore one more prosodic dimension, the historical. We must develop an awareness of large metrical contexts, traditions, and conventions, the kinds of contexts which we find firmly rooted in historical usage. One way to begin attaining this awareness is to consider the various kinds of prosodies or theoretical systems of meter which have prevailed during the history of the English language.

It is more accurate to speak of the history of English prosodies than of one English prosody, for historically considered the phenomena of English versification are too complex and multifold to be contained by any single system of explanation or description. Indeed, if we had to construct some generalizations that might hold true for all English poetry from, say, "The Battle of Maldon" in the tenth century to *Four Quartets* in the twentieth, it is doubtful that we could set forth more than the following three:

1. Because English is a much more accentual language than, for example, the Romance tongues, stress has generally played a more significant part in the structure of English verse than it has in many continental poetries.

2. The English language appears most naturally to organize

its rhythms in ascending patterns; that is, the main instinct in English poetry is for iambic or occasionally anapestic movements rather than for trochaic or dactylic.

3. Most English poetry seems to shape itself in lines of moderate length, lines with a strong propensity toward an uneven number of distinguishable time-units (i.e., five feet per line). We should not miss the suggestions of a norm implied by the fact that about three-quarters of all English poetry is in blank verse. It seems characteristic of the ear trained to Anglo-Saxon usages that, presented with a series of six- or seven-foot lines, it tends to break them down into smaller and presumably more manageable units (two threes; or fours and threes, as in ballad stanza). A long series of hexameters is significantly the metrical mode of the French, rather than the English, drama.

Other than sharing these three common characteristics, English poetries of various historical ages manifest few prosodic similarities. The distinguishing characteristics and conventions of the English prosodies are best seen if we consider them philologically or linguistically, that is, according to the state of the English language in various periods of its history.

OLD ENGLISH (c. A.D. 500–c. 1100): The powerful Germanic accents of the Old English language provide a natural basis for a very heavily accentual prosody in which sense rhythm rather than any abstract metrical imperative tends to supply the meter. The standard poetic line in Old English consists of four strongly stressed syllables arranged, together with any number of unstressed syllables, in two hemistichs (or half-lines) of two stresses each. Stressed syllables frequently alliterate, and the alliteration tends to emphasize even further the force of the accent. The overall organization of materials tends to be stichic rather than strophic—that is, we find an accumulation of lines in additive sequence rather than an organization of lines into short stanzas of significant shape. The two hemistichs which comprise the line are separated by an invariable medial caesura. Counterpoint or syncopation is achieved by occasional "rests" and the occasional omission of one of the four stressed syllables, especially in the second hemistich.

The following passage from *Beowulf* (lines 4–7) exemplifies the "normal" line structure (lines 1 and 2) and the possibilities for variation through rest and the omission of stress (lines 3 and 4) :

Oft Scýld Scéfing	scéaþena þréatum,
mónegum máegþum	méodsetla oftéah,
égsode eórlas	syþþan áerest wearþ
féasceaft fúnden	he þæs frófre gebad. . . .

[Often Scyld, the son of Sceaf, seized the mead-halls of many tribes; even though he had originally been discovered in a wretched state, he lived to find solace for that.]

John Collins Pope has conjectured that, in recitation, the normal position of the four stresses per line was signaled by a chord struck on a harp: this constant underlying beat would provide a sort of metrical underpinning against which the variations dictated by rhetorical emphasis would be counterpointed.

Old English versification presents a delusive air of simplicity: actually it is a metrical system of very subtle expressiveness, for its departures from the ideal meter and its often delightfully coy returns give the rhythm a constantly shifting surface bespeaking a high degree of sophistication. If, as Wimsatt and Beardsley find, Old English accentual meter has only a limited capacity for "interplay," most of the poets who have written in it have worked so skillfully that we hardly notice the limitations of the metrical system.

Some modern metrical critics and theorists have suggested that even beneath the iambic pentameter line of modern blank verse or of the heroic couplet we still catch a faint echo of the four-stress Old English line. And some have suggested that what we are talking about when we speak of "metrical variations" is really the line's apparent indecision about whether to adopt a four- or a five-stress structure—an indecision, we might say, about whether to "grow up" historically. As Joseph Malof says, "There is a significant tendency in the [iambic pentameter] line to lead a double life, to qualify for strict iambic pentameter through such devices as 'promotion' of a medial stress to the rank of a full one, and yet to assert beneath the surface the four strong beats of our native meter." But there is one difficulty with such theories—they tend to neglect the fact that, in the Old English line, structural alliteration and strong medial caesura are characteristics which are as strong as its four stresses: Modern English poetry has had no difficulty in casting off these other equally powerful characteristics of Old English verse.

Whatever the degree to which the modern iambic pentameter line "remembers" the stress scheme of Old English versification, these essentials of structural alliteration and invariable medial caesura pose problems to contemporary poets who now and then choose to exercise themselves in something like a reminiscence of the Old English mode. Most of W. H. Auden's *The Age of Anxiety* is written in a verse closely resembling the Old English accentual system, and now and then very pleasantly anachronistic effects result:

> . . . lightning at noonday
> Swiftly stooping to the summer-house
> Engraves its disgust on engrossed flesh,
> And at tea-times through tall french windows
> Hurtle anonymous hostile stones.
> No soul is safe. Let slight infection
> Disturb a trifle some tiny gland,
> And Caustic Keith grows kind and silly
> Or Dainty Daisy dirties herself.

It is all a very amusing but perhaps excessively self-conscious experience for both writer and reader.

A more successful suggestion of the tonality of Old English versification is possible when the poetic subject seems more appropriate. Richard Wilbur's "Junk," like Ezra Pound's "translations" from Old English, gives a contemporary twist to a favorite Old English subject, the power of good workmanship, and we end with a feeling that the spirits of two distinct ages have momentarily almost been joined:

> An axe angles
>   from my neighbor's ashcan;
> It is hell's handiwork,
>   the wood not hickory,
> The flow of the grain
>   not faithfully followed. . . .
>   . . . The heart winces

> For junk and gimcrack,
> > for jerrybuilt things
> And the men who make them
> > for a little money . . .
> They shall waste in the weather
> > towards what they were.
> The sun shall glory
> > in the glitter of glass-chips,
> Foreseeing the salvage
> > of the prisoned sand,
> And the blistering paint
> > peel off in patches,
> That the good grain
> > be discovered again.
> Then burnt, bulldozed,
> > they shall all be buried
> To the depth of diamonds,
> > in the making dark
> Where halt Hephæstus
> > keeps his hammer
> And Wayland's work
> > is worn away.

But ultimately we must conclude that, although Old English versification can be imitated, nothing really like it can be recovered: the language has changed, and each significant philological change projects us into an altered metrical world in which the meters of the past can be understood and appreciated but never again practiced.

MIDDLE ENGLISH (c. 1100–c. 1500) : After the Norman Conquest, the rapid changes in the language (loss of inflection, multiplication of dialects, Romance accretions to what had been primarily a Germanic vocabulary) quickly complicated and diversified the former stable and unitary prosody. Although it persisted for a time in the greatly changed language of Middle English, the old four-stress accentual line, with its varying number of unstressed syllables, was gradually abandoned in favor of a line in which, for the first time in English, syllabic numeration becomes an important structural criterion. The two hemistichs of the Old English line seem finally to metamorphose into the alternating four- and three-stress lines of the medieval ballad stanza. Strophic

construction begins to compete with stichic as a way of organizing poetic materials. The strongly Germanic accentual quality
of the language seems to weaken slightly, and instead of a prosody
based on emphatic pressures at approximately equal times we
find one expressive of a new consciousness of the qualitative
similarities between stressed and unstressed syllables.

The linguistic complexities of the Middle Ages created a situation in which several unique prosodies coexisted simultaneously.
Thus we find, as if competing for pre-eminence:

1. a continuation of the Old English four-stress accentual
prosody adapted (often by the addition of assonance and rhyme,
and by the rejection of the strong medial caesura) to the require-
ments of an increasingly less inflected language. Thus *Sir Gawain
and the Green Knight:*

> After, the sesoun of somer with the soft windes,
> When Zeferus sifles himself on sedes and erbes;
> Wela-winne is the wort that waxes theroute,
> When the donkande dewe dropes of the leves. . . .

2. accentual-syllabic rhyming verse in lines of four stresses and
eight syllables, gradually lengthening to approximate the heroic
couplets of Chaucer and Lydgate. An example is Chaucer's early
"Romance of the Rose":

> Ful gay was al the ground, and queint,
> And powdred, as men had it peint,
> With many a fressh and sondry flowr,
> That casten up ful good savour.

3. a highly accentual lyric prosody—sometimes over-stressed
until it resembles Hopkins's sprung rhythm—found especially in
songs and other pieces set to music. An example is the anonymous
fifteenth-century "I Sing of a Maiden":

> I sing of a maiden
>   That is makeles;
> King of alle kinges
>   To here sone che ches.
> [I sing of a maiden
>   Who knows no equal;
> The King of all Kings
>   For her son she chose.]

> He cam so stille,
> There his moder was,
> As dew in Aprille
> That fallith on the gras. . . .

Out of all this prosodic complication and variety, one tradition did gradually succeed in establishing preeminence: the accentual-syllabic. With the final relative stabilization of language and dialects long after the initial linguistic shock of the Conquest, the five-stress, decasyllabic line of Chaucer emerged: it is this line—the line that Chaucer can be said to have discovered for English poetry—which furnishes the base for Renaissance and later developments in Modern English.

MODERN ENGLISH *(c. 1500–)* : *Sixteenth and Seventeenth Centuries:* Three facts are important in Renaissance prosody: (1) the language attained a condition of relative stability; (2) the widespread admiration of the Greek and Latin classics invited imitation, and imitation served to expose the apparent coarseness of the English metric of preceding ages; and (3) rhetorical and metrical criticism, in the manner of the ancients, began to be written and read. There resulted a stream of systematic—and very often prescriptive—prosodic commentary which has continued without intermission to our own age.

The Renaissance admiration for Greek meters impelled one school of prosodists and poets to import Greek quantitative usages into English practice, and theorists, dilettantes, and poets like Ascham, Sidney, Spenser, and Campion labored, with varying seriousness and success, to imitate in English the classical heroic hexameter or the Greek lyric measures. But since the would-be quantitative poet was obliged to remember constantly the arbitrarily assigned "quantities" of the English syllables he chose to use, quantitative composition was a laborious academic-theoretical business, like all such nonempirical enterprises more gratifying to the self-congratulating practitioner than to the perplexed reader.

Along with this impulse to "refine" English verse by making it mimic classical rhythms went the development of the Chaucerian accentual-syllabic pentameter line as a vehicle for narrative and drama. The initial impulse was to urge the line toward a new regularity in stress placement, as Surrey and Sackville did, but soon a more civilized instinct for expressive variations made itself felt. Ironically, the regularists, by mistaking the whole aesthetic premise of meter, made their own unwitting contribution to the great English tradition of expressive metrical variations. As Joseph Malof has said, "The monotonously regular rhythms of the mid-sixteenth century were prerequisite to [the development of a feel for metrical variations] because they offered for the first time, in Tottel and in Gascoigne, the concept of a clear, workable metrical norm from which later poets were to make their prosperous departures." Among the most distinguished of those who soon mastered the art of "prosperous departures" were Marlowe and Shakespeare. Both use the accentual-syllabic pentameter with a consummate sensitivity, calmly inventing new tonalities when they have tired of the challenges of the old. And even the lesser dramatists of the age reveal, through their instinctive comfort within it, that the iambic pentameter is going to become, for whatever reason, the staple line of the Modern English period.

In lyric verse the song writers, obliged often to fit words to pre-existing airs, produced free accentual lines, and lyric practitioners like Donne, Crashaw, Herbert, and Marvell make of the iambic tetrameter or pentameter line a vehicle for wit, shock, and ecstasy by a bold shifting or addition of stresses.

And yet in the midst of all this happy inventiveness and flexibility we find already planted the seeds of an impulse toward greater prosodic regulation and predictability. Samuel Daniel's *Defense of Rhyme* (?1603) is a conservative prosodic document which anticipates and even invites the practice of such late seventeenth-century masters of the closed heroic couplet as Denham and Waller. In *Paradise Lost* Milton adheres quite consciously to a fixed decasyllabic limitation. The end of the Renaissance is thus coincident with a reaction against the metrical spontaneity of the Elizabethans: in both theory and practice, prosody is now moving toward an ideal of strict syllabic limitation in the line and even a relative predictability of stress positions.

Eighteenth Century: Prosody after the Restoration betrays a strong French syllabic influence: for a time, indeed, the essential criterion of the English poetic line ceases to be the number of either stresses or feet and becomes the number of syllables. Metrical theorists and dogmatists like Edward Bysshe, Richard

Bentley, and Henry Pemberton advocated a rigid regularity in the heroic line, and minor poets like Richard Glover responded by composing as far as they were able in a strictly regular accentual-syllabic verse without any expressive variations. This lust for regularity—"smoothness," the age was pleased to call it—seems to constitute one expression of the orderly and rationalistic impulses of the period. Although the best poets of the early eighteenth century (poets like Dryden, Prior, Gay, Swift, and Pope) largely maintained the Renaissance tradition of expressive variation, even they could not help responding to the regularistic climate: they carefully observed a uniformity in the number of syllables per line—that is, they were careful to use in substitution duple feet only—and they generally rejected the enjambed line in favor of a strict line integrity.

We can see what was happening if we compare a passage from Donne's "Fourth Satire" with a passage of what Pope called his "versification" of it. Donne speaks of a courtier thus:

> Therefore I suffer'd this; Towards me did run
> A thing more strange, than on Nile's slime, the Sun
> E'er bred, or all which into Noah's Ark came:
> A thing which would have pos'd Adam to name:

Notable in Pope's version is an impulse toward both stress regularity and greater line integrity: substitution, where it does occur, is permitted only at some distance from the line endings, which are reserved for strictly iambic assertions of the prevailing regularity:

> Scarce was I enter'd, when behold! there came
> A Thing which Adam had been pos'd to name;
> Noah had refus'd it lodging in his Ark,
> Where all the Race of Reptiles might embark.

Soon after 1740, however, another reaction set in: now it was a reaction against the very metrical neatness that Pope and his school had labored to refine. The reaction expressed itself in the prosodic writings of Samuel Say, John Mason, and Joshua Steele, who pointed out that monotony might easily be the cost of iambic lines long continued without trisyllabic substitution, and who argued that bold shifting and omission of stress are expressive techniques which the poet aspiring to exploit all the resources of metrical language cannot do without. The arguments of these critics of metrical regularity issue from a new and revolutionary aesthetic, one favoring impulse, spontaneity, and surprise rather than the Augustan values of stability, predictability, and quietude. Especially by opposing the poetic contractions necessitated by a strict accentual-syllabism, the late eighteenth-century metrical revolutionaries advocated an "expandable" line which could swell or diminish expressively according to the dynamics of the rhetorical pressures within it.

Unlike the prosodic theorizing and speculation of the Renaissance, which is still rather sparse, that of the eighteenth century is copious; it is also systematic, and, under the influence of the empiricism of John Locke, remarkably "psychological." Throughout the century the practice of the poets substantially follows the urgings of the conservative metrical theorists: although masters like Pope and Johnson shift stresses freely and instinctively, even they never violate the strict syllabic limitation—which means that they are careful to eschew trisyllabic substitution—and the lines of many lesser writers in the heroic couplet will be found to be strikingly regular in the alternate disposition of stressed and unstressed syllables.

Nineteenth Century: The great phenomenon in nineteenth-century English versification is the rejection of strict accentual-syllabism in favor of accentualism. This is to say that the use of trisyllabic substitution in duple metrical contexts becomes the technical hallmark of the age, just as the careful avoidance of trisyllabic substitution had been the rhythmical sign of eighteenth-century poetry. In his "Christabel" Coleridge publicly practiced—and for a wide audience—the principles of trisyllabic substitution advocated a half-century earlier by Say, Mason, and Steele. As a result of this new aspiration toward accentualism, the English pentameter line tends to lose its Augustan formal and oratorical tone and to assume an air of an almost colloquial intimacy, varying from the sober sincerity of the verse of "The Prelude" to the racy energy of the verse of "Fra Lippo Lippi." In prosodic theorizing, the impulse toward accentualism manifests itself in the development of musical analogies to verse and in musical methods of scansion: Sidney Lanier is a pioneer in this work. And the cause of accentualism was bolstered by the rise to academic fashion of Germanic philology, which served to remind both prosodists and poets that English was solidly a Germanic tongue whose metrical basis must be primarily some arrangement of strong accents. Indeed, the transfer of British intellectual allegiance from France to Germany during the nineteenth century can be deduced in part from the British rediscovery of the charms of accentual versification. But an impatience with inherited metrical restraints is probably the clearest motive underlying the metrical behavior of nineteenth-century poets: the development of "free verse" around the middle of the century was conceived by many—and may be conceived by us—as an expression of nineteenth-century liberalism or of the primitivist strain of romanticism. Another unique nineteenth-century prosodic phenomenon is the attempt to enlist triple base-rhythms in support of nonfrivolous subjects, as Longfellow, Poe, and Swinburne tried to do.

But despite the general atmosphere of mild experimentation, many of the most prominent practitioners, like Tennyson and Arnold, continued to work in what is fundamentally the accentual-syllabic line bequeathed them by the Augustans, with its strict syllabic limitation and its conservative placement of stresses. At the close of the century, it is true, W. J. Stone tried to urge the more academic spirits toward quantitative prosody once more, but the gradual decay of classical learning and enthusiasm—and the increasing association of classical learning with mere gentility—practically guaranteed a tiny and ineffective audience for such Alexandrian pursuits. It was at this time that Hopkins was moved to experiment with his technique of overstressing, which bespeaks its historical context once we perceive how intimately it partakes in the prevailing accentual rhythmical climate and even in the widespread Victorian admiration for all things Germanic.

The main nineteenth-century divagation from accentual-syllabism and the air of genteel quest and experimentation suggest also a current of dissatisfaction with the sound of conservative verse, and this dissatisfaction may have some philological cause. For example, the gradual secession of the American from the British dialects may be connected with the simultaneous British search for new metrical tonalities. The gradual replacement of classical by modern-language studies in schools and universities may also bespeak a subtle alteration in linguistic habits and rhythmical tastes. Whatever the causes and the meaning of the metrical restlessness of many nineteenth-century poets, the restlessness is clearly one expression of their lust for liberal reform and their commitment to the idea of progress.

Twentieth Century: Brooding over the metrical history of our time is the spirit of one of the greatest of traditional accentual-syllabic metrists, William Butler Yeats. It is the force of his example as a poet of rich traditional metrical usages that, time and again, has brought contemporary poets back to the practice of accentual-syllabism after experimental excursions in other prosodic systems, or after vacations in none at all. Most of the temporary prosodic mutations which have taken place in the twentieth century have been associated with the United States rather than with Britain: perhaps one reason is the greater accessibility to American poets of the fructifying, revolutionary example of Whitman. During the 1920's and 1930's, Ezra Pound and William Carlos Williams tightened the freely cadenced long line of Whitman and made of it a witty, informal instrument for registering the rhythms of actual American speech. T. S. Eliot's poetic dramas have shown what can still be done with a quiet, subtle accentualism, and W. H. Auden has written accentual, accentual-syllabic, and syllabic verse with equal facility. But even such engaging American experiments as the "spatial cadences" of E. E. Cummings and the cadenced syllabism of Marianne Moore have stimulated no great horde of precise followers and exploiters. Or to put it more accurately: their followers have conspicuously lacked the metrical learning and inventiveness of the American masters of the 1920's and 1930's. Many modern American and British poets, after canvassing the possibilities of an apparently "freer" metric, have returned to a more or less stable sort of Yeatsian accentual-syllabism: Frost, the Stevens of "Sunday Morning," Robert Graves, James Merrill, Richard Wilbur, Randall Jarrell, and W. D. Snodgrass have all turned from the metrical radicalism of the 1920's and gravitated toward the accentual-syllabism which, for over four centuries, has been the staple system for poetry in Modern English. How closely a return like this to "the tradition" in metrics is connected with a similar conservative movement in general intellectual taste it would be hard to say. It will be obvious, however, to those who can see in history the very intimate alliance between metrics and the larger intellectual and emotional conventions of an age that no prosodic phenomenon is devoid of wider meaning if only we read it correctly.

When we stand well back and survey the whole history of English versification over almost fifteen centuries, we perceive even through the philological upheavals a recurring pattern. The pattern described by metrical history is similar, perhaps, to the general shape of political history in that it consists of oscillations now toward ideals of tight control and unitary domination and now toward a relaxation of such control and domination. But metrical history differs from political in one important way: while political history can be shown to involve a very gradual total tendency toward, say, ideals of egalitarianism or public philanthropy, metrical history exhibits no such long-term "progressive" tendency. Meter has not really become "freer" over the centuries, and indeed "freedom" is not a virtue in meter—expressiveness is. The metrical imperative underlying the words that Yeats arranges is hardly less rigid and "perfect" than that underlying Chaucer's poetic discourse; and in "free verse" that works there are imperatives no less visible.

There will always be those to say with Jane Heap, one of the editors of the *Little Review* between the two World Wars, "A new age has created a new kind of beauty," and who will imagine that the essential conventions of a given art can "progress" or even change drastically as if in response to technological change. But the problem is knowing when a really new age, rather than an apparently new one, has dawned. A "new age" for metrics is a new philological age, not a new technological one: essential changes in the structure of the English language cannot be willed, and it is such essential changes that a new metrical system tends to reflect.

Artistic progressives like Jane Heap seem always destined for defeat in the long run by two facts of life: (1) Modern English is Modern English and not, philologically, something else; and (2) the modern reader of poetry in English, despite his vast difference in extrinsic and learned attitudes from, say, his Elizabethan counterpart, has still the same kind of physique and personal physiological rhythms as his forebears. These will still seem to seek satisfaction and delight in ways which accord with the experienced rhythmic traditions of Modern English. If these traditions should ever become totally irrecoverable, it would not be pleasant to calculate what will be lost forever.

5

Free Verse

The main nineteenth- and twentieth-century departure from traditional systems of metrical regularity deserves a
chapter by itself. The first problem is the very term *free verse*.
If we are persuaded with T. S. Eliot that "there is no freedom
in art," the term *free verse* will strike us as a flagrant oxymoron.
But if *free verse* seems an affront to logic, the term has the merit
of familiarity and is thus handier than the pedantic *cadenced
verse* or the awkward *non-metrical verse* or the pretentious *vers
libre*. We will use *free verse,* but we will want to be aware that
free has approximately the status it has in the expression *Free
World*. That is, free, sort of.

Another problem is that the designation *free verse* seems to
imply something clearly distinguishable. But free verse is a
matter of degree. Just as accentual-syllabic verse with abundant
trisyllabic substitutions shades into accentual verse, so, if the
number of stresses per line is not uniform or predictable, accentual verse shades into free verse. In the same way, as it leaves
behind—like much contemporary poetry—the sense of the line
as a strong element of pattern, free verse shades into rhythmical
prose. But even if the term *free verse* is not precise, it is precise
enough to distinguish the essential method of post-Yeatsian verse
in general. Whatever it is, a poetic medium must be more than
a faddish "relaxation" of a former convention if it has served
as the medium of major achievements by such undoubted modern

masters as Wallace Stevens, Ezra Pound, T. S. Eliot, William Carlos Williams, and D. H. Lawrence. Whatever it means, *free verse* designates the modern style, and anyone aspiring to experience the permanent masterpieces of modern poetry must achieve some understanding of its techniques.

"It is no use inventing fancy laws for free verse," says D. H. Lawrence, and we can agree. But an empirical study of thousands of free-verse poems will lead any reader to some generalizations by way of definition. Like other distinguishable verse mediums, free verse—despite its name—follows its own more-or-less strict imperatives. Two of these are instantly obvious to ear and eye. The free-verse poem establishes a texture without metrical regularity—measurable meter is as much an anomaly in a free-verse poem as the want of it is in a metered poem. And most free-verse poems eschew rhyme as well. One reason Ogden Nash's poems are funny, indeed, is that they offer studiously self-conscious rhymes in an un-metrical texture where we have been taught not to expect rhyme. For example, the beginning of "The Terrible People":

People who have what they want are very fond of telling people who
    haven't what they want that they really don't want it,
And I wish I could afford to gather all such people into a gloomy
    castle on the Danube and hire half a dozen capable Draculas to
    haunt it.
I don't mind their having a lot of money, and I don't care how they
    employ it,
But I do think they damn well ought to admit they enjoy it.

Other imperatives honored by many modern free-verse practitioners are more mechanically typographical or orthographical: abandoning the tradition that each poetic line begins with a capital, for example; or forsaking punctuation; or exhibiting a just-folks idiosyncrasy in informal abbreviations like *i.e.* and *etc.*, or like Pound's *sez, shd, wd, sd, yr, cd* for *says, should, would, said, your,* and *could;* or using every symbol on the typewriter, like *&* and the equals sign; or using things like " (!) ," which would surely defeat the most resolute scanner of a standard metrical line.

Other traditions of free verse work to determine the conduct and often the theme of the whole poem. As Theodore Roethke observes, the technique of enumeration or catalog has been standard in free verse since early Hebrew practice, as in *Job*, where the Lord runs through a catalog of items indicating Job's ignorance and weakness:

> Will the unicorn be willing to serve thee, or abide by thy crib?
>
> . . .
>
> Gavest thou the goodly wings unto the peacocks? or wings and feathers unto the ostrich?
>
> . . .
>
> Hast thou given the horse strength? hast thou clothed his neck with thunder?
>
> . . .
>
> Does the hawk fly by thy wisdom, and stretch her wings toward the south?
> Doth the eagle mount up at thy command, and make her nest on high?
>
> (39:9, 13, 19, 26–27)

In the middle of the eighteenth century Christopher Smart catalogued the attributes of his cat Jeoffrey in free-verse lines recalling those of the Old Testament or of Christian liturgy:

> For having done duty and received blessing he begins to consider himself.
> For this he performs in ten degrees.
> For first he looks upon his fore-paws to see if they are clean.
> For secondly he kicks up behind to clear away there.
> For thirdly he works it upon stretch with the fore paws extended.
> For fourthly he sharpens his paws by wood.
> For fifthly he washes himself,

and so on up to

> For tenthly he goes in quest of food.

> (*Jubilate Agno*)

If the catalogs of ancient epic seem to lie behind the heroic enumerations in the Ossianic prose-poems of Smart's contemporary James Macpherson and in Blake's loose-lined Prophetic Books, Whitman's enumerations intimate a sometimes astonishing equality in the things catalogued, and we get a foreshadowing of the often ironic juxtapositions of *The Waste Land* and the *Cantos*:

The pure contralto signs in the organ loft,
The carpenter dresses his plank . . .
The duck-shooter walks by cautious and silent stretches,
The deacons are ordain'd with cross'd hands at the altar . . .
The connoisseur peers along the exhibition-gallery with half-shut eyes
    bent sideways,
As the deck-hands make fast the steamboat the plank is thrown for the
    shore-going passengers. . . .

And then one of Whitman's happiest near-juxtapositions:

The prostitute draggles her shawl, her bonnet bobs on her tipsy and
    pimpled neck, . . .
The President holding a cabinet council is surrounded by the great
    secretaries.

(Song of Myself, 15)

As Roethke is aware, enumeration, "the favorite device of the
more irregular poem," is the method of his "Elegy for Jane,"
which begins, he points out, " 'I remember,' then the listing":

I remember the neckcurls, limp and damp as tendrils;
And her quick look, a sidelong pickerel smile;
And how, once startled into talk, the light syllables leaped for her,
And she balanced in the delight of her thought . . .

Enumeration is the essential method of countless other modern
free-verse poems, from Ginsberg's *Howl* to Irving Feldman's "The
Pripet Marshes." With a series of loose un-metrical lines beginning "Maury is there," "And Frank," "And blonde Lettie," "And
Marian," "And Adele," "And my red-haired sisters," Feldman
catalogs the inhabitants of a Jewish village in the Ukraine just
before the Germans arrive. He catalogs them and stabilizes them
within the theater of his poem in order to save them. Just before
the Germans wheel into town, he says, "I snatch them all back."
   As these examples indicate, free-verse lines, deprived of pattern
in one dimension, the metrical, tend to compensate by employing
another kind of pattern, conspicuous repetition of phrases or
syntactical forms. A special kind of significant repetition is almost the hallmark of a certain school of modern free verse.
Consider D. H. Lawrence's "The English Are So Nice," which

in its 22 lines repeats *nice* (or *nicer* and *nicest*) 17 times, or Whitman's 13-line "Tears," which repeats *tears* 12 times. A more subtle example is Whitman's "Beginning My Studies":

> Beginning my studies the first step pleas'd me so much,
> The mere fact consciousness, these forms, the power of motion,
> The least insect or animal, the senses, eyesight, love,
> The first step I say awed me and pleas'd me so much,
> I have hardly gone and hardly wish'd to go any farther,
> But stop and loiter all the time to sing it in ecstatic songs.

With that we can compare Lawrence's four-line "Self-Pity":

> I never saw a wild thing
> sorry for itself.
> A small bird will drop frozen dead from a bough
> without ever having felt sorry for itself.

Phrasal repetitions occurring at the beginnings of lines, the most common kind of repetition we find in free verse, create an effect called, formally, *anaphora:*

> Out of the cradle endlessly rocking,
> Out of the mocking-bird's throat, the musical shuttle,
> Out of the Ninth-month midnight, . . .

Because in free verse the length of the line is determined by feel rather than established pattern, a crucial problem for the poet is knowing when to break lines. "I think very few people can manage free verse," says Auden. "You need an infallible ear, like D. H. Lawrence, to determine where the lines should end." And two possibilities in the treatment of line-endings suggest two ultimate kinds of free verse. One kind, which John Hollander designates the oracular, exhibits unvarying line integrity, often with anaphora, as in Ginsberg's *Howl* or much of the more formal Whitman:

> Welcome are all earth's lands, each for its kind,
> Welcome are lands of pine and oak,
> Welcome are lands of the lemon and fig,
> Welcome are lands of gold . . .
>   (*Song of the Broad-Axe*)

The effect is that of public speaking. But if constant enjambment takes place—that is, if the sense and syntax of one line
run on into the next so that a hearer would have trouble ascertaining the line breaks—we have a very different kind of free
verse, a kind we can designate as meditative and ruminative or
private. It is this kind of vigorously enjambed free verse which
has become a common style in the last twenty years or so as a
vehicle for themes that are sly or shy, or uncertain, or quietly
ironic, or furtive. W. C. Williams, Frank O'Hara, Robert Bly,
Robert Creeley, William Merwin are adepts at this style. To
Whitman's line-by-line public proclamations above we can contrast Williams's run-on domestic confessional "note":

THIS IS JUST TO SAY

> I have eaten
> the plums
> that were in
> the icebox
>
> and which
> you were probably
> saving
> for breakfast
>
> Forgive me
> they were delicious
> so sweet
> and so cold

One thing notable here is the way the title itself "runs on"
into the opening: the illusion is that the poem is so magically
organic that not even a part traditionally considered separable
can distance itself. This device seems by now almost obligatory in
a certain kind of enjambed free verse which aims at wit. For
example, Marianne Moore:

THE MONKEYS

> winked too much and were afraid of snakes . . .

Robert Kelly:

THE BOAT

floated in the cove . . .

Marvin Bell:

HERE

on Venus, time passes slowly . . .

Tess Gallagher:

THE HORSE IN THE DRUGSTORE

wants to be admired.

Clearly, "free verse" can manage every tone from the pompously ceremonial to the apologetically informal. But this is not to imply that as a technique whose flowering is associated with American intellectual and emotional configurations in the mid-nineteenth century, free verse does not itself seem to generate certain specific themes, which such devices as unpredictable line-length and unadvertised rhythms seem to trigger. From the beginnings of its development by Whitman, the subtle rhythmic patterns discernible in sequences of free-verse lines have been likened to sea-waves, it being widely assumed in Whitman's time that the "natural" rather than the artificial and conventional is what governs the imperatives of art. To Whitman, the sea itself is a great free-verse poem, whose "lines" are "the liquid, billowy waves, ever rising and falling, perhaps wild with storm, always moving, always alike in their nature as rolling waves, but hardly any two exactly alike in size or measure." In theme as well as theory, free verse has shown an affinity with the sea, inviting us to trace a thematic tradition from Whitman's "Out of the Cradle Endlessly Rocking" all the way to A. R. Ammons's "Corson's Inlet," with stops along the way at Lawrence's "The Sea," Robinson Jeffers's "Night" and "November Surf," and Marianne Moore's "A Grave." When we consider literary history it seems no accident that the nineteenth- and twentieth-century discovery of the sea as a useful emblem of infinity or freedom or wonder and the seashore as a venue of illumination is virtually coincident with the rise to popularity of free verse.

Ammons's "Corson's Inlet" (1965) is an instructive example of this apparently natural alliance between technique and theme. This quiet, meditative poem consists of 128 enjambed lines, varying in length from one to fifteen syllables. The rhythm sounds like that of well-written prose. But the repetitions we expect in free verse are here, and they involve words implying the relation of verse-form to theme in this poem, words like *walk, order, lines, forms,* and *shape.* The action of the poem is a desultory stroll along the New Jersey shore, and the point is that to trace the natural shoreline with its rounded, unplanned contours is to understand at once both a valuable intellectual and emotional range of possibilities and a verse-form which can render them suggestively. As the speaker says,

> the walk liberating, I was released from forms,
> from the perpendiculars,
> > straight lines, blocks, boxes, binds
> of thought
> into the hues, shadings, rises, flowing bends and blends of sight:

> > I allow myself eddies of meaning:

Because, as the speaker finds,

> in nature there are few sharp lines,

in thought and poems there should be few either:

> I have reached no conclusions, have erected no boundaries,
> shutting out and shutting in, separating inside
> > from outside: I have
> > drawn no lines: . . .

Just as his thought is instructed by the informal curvings the sea has made in the inlet, so the speaker's lines wax and wane, extend and contract, running on freely. They reject the "limited tightness" of a preordained metrical scheme, and we feel that for bodying forth this theme, at least, Ammons's loose texture is nicely appropriate.

In a similar way, the free-verse technique of Whitman's *Song of Myself* seems virtually to determine that the theme of the poem will be "freedom" and flux as distinguished from the enclosing "houses and rooms" of traditional metrical lines and poetic forms. Related themes that likewise seem prompted by free-verse technique are the delights of wandering (Whitman's *Song of the Open Road*) and the unexpected value of the lowly (*Song of Myself*, Section 5; W. C. Williams, *Spring and All*), revealed by informal but precise scrutiny of common particulars. Again, the way free verse "moves" apparently without predictable constraints seems to establish it as a natural style for vignettes of imagistic kinesis like Whitman's "Cavalry Crossing a Ford" or Cummings's "All in green went my love riding." Robert Bly's free-verse horses, as well as his free-verse automobile drives, are in the tradition.

Because successful free verse generally avoids the illusion of stresses arranged in some form of patterned repetition, it probably cannot be scanned, but it can certainly be analyzed and appraised, and its rhythmic movements, even if subtle, can be judged as reinforcements or impediments of the progress of idea and feeling. Many free-verse poems operate traditionally to this degree: that they establish a non- or anti-metrical verbal continuum as a grid against which occasional metrical moments are perceived as especially forceful. An example is Whitman's "When I Heard the Learn'd Astronomer," which devotes seven lines to establishing a loose "sincere" quasi-prosaic grid as a field against which the remarkably regular final line of iambic pentameter emerges with special emphasis reinforcing the irony:

When I heard the learn'd astronomer,
When the proofs, the figures, were ranged in columns before me,
When I was shown the charts and diagrams, to add, divide, and
    measure them,
When I sitting heard the astronomer where he lectured with much
    applause in the lecture-room,
How soon unaccountable I became tired and sick,
Till rising and gliding out I wander'd off by myself,
In the mystical moist night-air, and from time to time

—and then the shock of regular iambic pentameter registering a different and more valid way of perceiving:

> Look'd up in perfect silence at the stars.

This poem might be taken to illustrate Roethke's view that "free verse is a denial in terms." As he says, the reason is that "there is, invariably, the ghost of some other form, often blank verse, behind what is written." One way of analyzing Whitman's poem as a rhythmical phenomenon is to suggest that the final line discloses the ghost meter which the poem has been concealing all along.

It goes without saying that when a free-verse poem does surprise us by introducing a moment of recognizable traditional rhythm, such a rhythm should be related to meaning. As it almost always is in masters like Whitman and Pound. Consider Whitman's frequent presentation of an amphibrachic foot ($\smile/\smile$) at the ends of his long free-verse lines, where he seems at pains to remind the reader rhythmically of the sound of the classical heroic hexameter, the traditional medium of old-style "epic." Here in *Song of Myself*, Whitman's proposal for a new kind of lyric-epic, he contrives that the loose rhythms of each line shall clarify to a terminal amphibrach, and we are to gather that Whitman, if not a new Homer, is at least a better Longfellow:

> The day getting ready for me when I shall do as much good as the best,
>   and be as/ prŏdígiŏus;/
> By my life-lumps! becoming already a/ crĕátŏr,/
> Putting myself here and now to the ambush'd womb of/ thĕ shádŏws./

Pound behaves similarly in his version of lyric-epic, the *Cantos*. It is to his advantage too to remind us of the atmosphere of traditional epic, especially the *Odyssey*, and although his prevailing medium is largely free verse, he deviates from it into frequent terminal amphibrachs:

> In the gloom, the gold gathers the light/ ăgaínst ĭt./

And here the Odyssean note:

> The boat's sails hung loose at/thĕ moórĭng,/
> Cloud like a sail/ĭnvértĕd./

But usually the free-verse poet's ambition is less to exhibit meter than to keep it from showing. He has numerous other methods for reinforcing sense, methods resembling those by which a writer in traditional meter "syncopates" by executing significant variations on established patterns. One way the free-verse practitioner can exploit the device of varying from a norm is to offer a long line against a preceding grid of short ones, or a short line after we've got accustomed to long ones. The latter is what, sixty-nine years old and paralyzed, Whitman does in his little autobiographical poem "The Dismantled Ship." Here the first four lines establish a medium which expands with each line. The syllables grow from 10 in the first line to 12 in the second, then to 14, and then to 20. But the anticlimactic final line contracts to six syllables, and its two stresses follow a line of ten: we get the point about the contraction of possibility and realize why the ship has been depicted as *gray* and *disabled:*

> In some unused lagoon, some nameless bay,
> On sluggish, lonesome waters, anchor'd near the shore,
> An old, dismasted, gray and batter'd ship, disabled, done,
> After free voyages to all the seas of earth, haul'd up at last and
>   hawser'd tight,
> Lies rusting, mouldering.

Just as the diaphragm of a camera lens opens up to admit more light or closes down to exclude it, so the openings and closings of many free-verse poems gradually expand or contract line-lengths to admit us to the vision or to dismiss us. Whitman is fond of opening poems by systematically expanding lines this way: the first three lines of "Crossing Brooklyn Ferry" contain 11, 18, and then 22 syllables:

> Flood-tide below me! I see you face to face!
> Clouds of the west—sun there half an hour high—I see you also face to
>   face.

Crowds of men and women attired in the usual costumes, how curious
   you are to me!

In "On the Beach at Night" Whitman opens the diaphragm to
let the scene in with lines of first 5, then 7, and finally 8 syllables:

   On the beach at night,
   Stands a child with her father,
   Watching the east, the autumn sky.

In the same way, "When I Heard the Learn'd Astronomer"
gradually reveals the scene in the lecture-room by offering first
a line of 9 syllables, then one of 14, then a third expanding to 18.
   This device of expanding lines to register expanding sense
Whitman exploits within poems as well, as in *Song of Myself*,
Section 20, where the expansion of the understanding through
the perception of accumulated figures reflects itself in the expansion of the lines from 6, to 18, to 19 syllables:

I know I am deathless,
I know this orbit of mine cannot be swept by a carpenter's compass,
I know I shall not pass like a child's carlacue cut with a burnt stick at
   night.

And Whitman can close down as effectively by shortening lines
as if stopping down the diaphragm. Thus the end of *Song of
Myself:*

   Failing to fetch me at first keep encouraged,   (11)
   Missing me one place search another,   (9)
   I stop somewhere waiting for you.   (8)

It is a strategy belonging less to Whitman, perhaps, than to free
verse in general, as Roethke indicates when, discussing his "Elegy
for Jane," he points to the way "the last three lines in the [first]
stanza lengthen out":

   The shade sang with her;
   The leaves, their whispers turned to kissing;
   And the mold sang in the bleached valleys under the rose.

"A kind of continuing triad," says Roethke. "In the last two stanzas exactly the opposite occurs, the final lines being,

> Over this damp grave I speak the words of my love:
> I, with no rights in this matter,
> Neither father nor lover."

From these examples we can infer that a free-verse poem without dynamics—without, that is, perceptible interesting movement from one given to another or without significant variations from some norm established by the texture of the poem—will risk the same sort of dullness as the metered poem which never varies from regularity. When it solicits our attention as poetry, a group of words arranged at apparent haphazard is as boring as *tum-ti-tum*.

A lot of people take the term *free verse* literally, with the result that there is more bad free verse written today than one can easily shake a stick at. Most of it hopes to recommend itself by deploying vaguely surrealistic images in unmetered colloquial idiom to urge acceptable opinions: that sex is a fine thing, that accurate perception is better than dull, that youth is probably a nicer condition than age, that there is more to things than their appearances; as well as that Lyndon Johnson and Richard Nixon were war criminals, that the C.I.A. is a menace, that corporations are corrupt, that contemporary history seems "entropic," and that women get a dirty deal. All very true and welcome. Yet what is lamentably missing is the art that makes poems re-readable once we have fathomed what they "say."

Indeed, free verse without subtle dynamics has become the received, standard contemporary style, as John Hollander notices: "At the present time in the United States, there is a widespread, received free-verse style marked by a narrow (25-30 em) format, strong use of line-ending as a syntactical marker, etc., which plays about the same role in the ascent to paradise as the received Longfellow style did a century ago." Or, we can add, as the received mechanical heroic-couplet style two centuries ago. But the principle of excellence in each of these styles is the same, and it can be perceived and enjoyed by anyone who will take a little time. The principle is that every technical gesture in a poem must justify itself in meaning. Which is to say that the free-verse writer can proclaim, with Ammons, that he is "released from forms," but he'd better not be. In free verse the abandonment of capital letters and punctuation must say something consonant with what the predications in the poem are saying. The sudden shortening of a line must say something. The degree of line-integrity or enjambment must refract the rhetorical status of the poem's address. And any momentary deviation into meter must validate itself, must appear not a lapse but a significant bold stroke. For the reader to attend to things like these may be harder than for him to respond to, say, a skillfully reversed foot in a metered line. But he must learn to attend to them if he is to take a pleasure less doctrinal than artistic in the poetry of his own time.

6

Some Critical Implications of Metrical Analysis

Until we have ventured to bring it to bear upon the evaluation of a whole poem, we cannot say that we have really done anything worth doing with metrical analysis. Prosodic study justifies itself only as an adjunct to criticism, and it is time now to advance and to test some fundamental critical principles.

In the appraisal of poetry an axiom perhaps generally accepted is that, given a poetic subject and treatment that "work"—that is, that stand a good chance of engaging repeatedly the best wits of a good reader—and given the benefits of an accurate taste in the contrivance and disposition of its metaphors, a poem stands a chance of attaining greater success and permanence the nearer it approaches absolute economy and coherence of the parts that comprise it. What is wanted is the closest possible approximation of absolute density. For the texture of a poem must be dense: when old-fashioned critics assert that in a poem every vein must be rifted with ore, that is what, in their quaint way, they mean. Density of texture is attained by an interweaving of poetic elements—predications, metaphors, rhythm—so firmly and tightly that, once interwoven, the separate strands resist unraveling, and, as it were, transform themselves into each other.

From this initial axiom of economy and coherence we can deduce the first of our general critical principles: The meter of a poem, no matter how extrinsically discovered and traditionally exploited by the poet, should give the illusion of having arisen intrinsically and subtly from within the uniqueness of the poetic occasion. Specifically, within the conventions of a given poetic period, there are some subjects and approaches that better suit, say, free verse or loose blank verse than tight blank verse, or the heroic couplet than anapestic tetrameter triplets. A master is one whose practice persuades us that his general metrical choice is the only thinkable one for his poem. And here again, what succeeds is less what accords with abstract principle than what works on the reader: the art of poetry is the art of illusion, and the illusion that succeeds in delighting and illuminating the subtle and trained reader is what we want, no matter how many "rules" are violated or received idols shattered.

It is in the light of this first critical principle that we must reject effects of appliquéd metrical regularity. Here we are given the illusion that the things in the poem are yielding excessively to external pressure, the way when we are riding alone on a train our thoughts tend to turn mere victims of the clicking of the wheels. What appears to have happened when a poem manifests an excessively regular metric is that one of its many elements, the metrical, has hypertrophied and stands in a gross and unlovely imbalance to the rest. This defect seems apparent in something like Browning's "Love Among the Ruins":

> Where the quiet-coloured end of evening smiles
> > Miles and miles
> On the solitary pastures where our sheep
> > Half-asleep
> Tinkle homeward thro' the twilight, stray or stop
> > As they crop—
> Was the site once of a city great and gay,
> > (So they say)
> Of our country's very capital, its prince
> > Ages since
> Held his court in, gathered councils, wielding far
> > Peace or war.

Dancing, anyone? Here indeed the coarseness of the metric seems quite a function of the banality of the rest of the texture ("a city great and gay"; "our country's very capital"), and in this melancholy sense the meter could almost be said to be organic with the

other textural elements, elements which seem the very antithesis
of the ideal of density.

An excessively "imposed" meter, although defective, becomes
more interesting the nearer the meter approaches something like
appropriateness. Thus the insufficiently varied, "external" meter
of Poe's "Annabel Lee" might be partially justified by the fictive
speaker's rural simplicity: he is uttering a sort of first-person
ballad, and the speaker capable of syntax like

> . . . this maiden she lived with no other thought
> Than to love and be loved by me

is surely no inappropriate contriver of primitive rhythms like

> . . . the moon never beams without bringing me dreams
> Of the beautiful Annabel Lee.

But even here we cannot avoid concluding that the poet, while
pretending to entice us into the world of poetry, has actually
admitted us only to the world of the popular song. Nineteenth-
century poets exploiting triple meters for exotic effects—the Poe
of "Ulalume" is a pre-eminent example—seem especially likely to
produce work in which the meter has this overlaid, imposed
quality, to create poems in which the insistent banging on the big
bass drum enfeebles all the other instruments and finally drives
the audience home with a headache.

And it is not only triple meters that seduce the unwary poet
into an imposed metrical regularity: iambic pentameter exerts its
own kind of beguilements. In pentameter there is a universe of
difference between a hapless or automatic regularity and an expressive one; between, say, the regularity of these lines from
John Bidlake's "The Country Parson,"

> With heart compact as truth the cabbage stands,
> With trickling gems bedropt in twinkling play;
> There nodding onions rang'd like marshall'd bands.
> The sluggard carrot sleeps his days in bed;
> The crippled pea alone that cannot stand;
> With vegetable marrow, rich and grand,

and the regularity of the crucial line of Wordsworth's "Michael,"

Ănd név/ĕr líft/ĕd úp/ă sín/glĕ stóne,/

which, terminating as it does a painful domestic episode that has been enacted in a fully varied blank verse, serves to transmit a reinforcement of the monotony to which the lonely peasant, in his old age, is irrevocably destined.

It is a similar kind of expressive rather than automatic regularity that Milton achieves at the end of *Paradise Lost.* After twelve books exhibiting the most lavish metrical variations, Milton elects to end the poem on a note of calm regularity, a regularity suggesting, not without a touch of melancholy for the glory that Adam and Eve have lost forever, a more rational, perhaps a more human, kind of hope:

> Sóme nát/ural tears they dropp'd, but wiped them soon;
> The World was all before them, where to choose
> Thir place of rest, and Pro/vĭdĕnce/ thir guide:
> Théy hánd/in hand, with wand'ring steps and slow
> Through Eden took thir solitary way.

Remembering that *natural* in line 1 is reduced by syncope to *nat'ral*, we find here only three substitutions in five lines: initial spondees in lines 1 and 4, and a pyrrhic in the fourth position of line 3. We should not neglect to admire the expressive force of the spondee which opens line 4 and which rhythmically foreshadows the "slow" steps which the latter part of the line depicts. These five closing lines are a remarkable show of regularity for Milton, and his art and taste are such that his presentation of a regular meter here is as stunning and meaningful as his customary reliance on a more splendidly varied one.

To compare George Crabbe frigid with George Crabbe afire is to get a fairly accurate feel for what is fatally defective about a metrical regularity that arises less from the real pressure and meaning of the poetic moment than from a reminiscence of other poems or from a sense of painful duty toward a presumed abstract "rule." Here the twenty-one-year-old Crabbe jingles away in "Inebriety":

> But cease, my Muse; of those or these enough,
> The fools who lis/tĕn, ănd/the knaves who scoff;
> The jest profane, that mocks th'offended God,
> Defies his power, and sets at nought his rod;
> The empty laugh, discretion's vainest foe,
> From fool to fool re-echo'd to and fro;
> The sly Indecency, that slowly springs
> From barren wit, and halts on trembling wings:
> Enough of these, and all the charms of Wine;
> Be sober joys and social evenings mine.

Except for the one pyrrhic in line 2—a traditional substitution popularized by Pope for this symmetrical compound phrasing—these ten lines exhibit no substitution, and we get the feeling that the metrical regularity is sanctioned by nothing in the passage itself: on the contrary, indeed, it is the very irregularity of drunkenness that constitutes the focus and that seems to call out for metrical demonstration: we remember Charles Cotton's drunkard and his energetic trochaic sweating. Crabbe's meter thus remains an inert appliqué.

But contrast what happens in "The Village," written a mere eight years later:

> Lo! where the heath, with withering brake grown o'er,
> Lénds thĕ/líght túrf/that warms the neighbouring poor;
> From thence a length of burning sand appears,
> Where the/thín hár/vest waves its wither'd ears;
> Ránk wéeds,/that every art and care defy,   5
> Réign ŏ'er/the land, and rob the blighted rye;
> There thistles stretch their prickly arms afar,
> And to the ragged infant threaten war;
> There poppies, nodding, mock the hope of toil;
> There the/blúe bú/gloss paints the sterile soil;   10
> Hárdÿ/and high, above the slender sheaf,
> The slimy mallow waves her silky leaf;
> O'er the/yóung shóot/the charlock throws a shade,
> And clasping tares/clíng róund/the sicky blade;
> With mingled tints the rocky coasts abound,   15
> And a sad splendour vainly shines around.

Here the counterpointing at the beginnings of lines, especially lines 2, 5, 6, and 11, serves to reinforce the shock of the successive revelations; and the medial spondees (lines 2, 4, 10, 13, 14) organically reinforce both the irony of the speaker's response to an overtly hostile nature (lines 2 and 4) and the unremitting vigor of that hostility (lines 10 and 14). Where we are presented with a regular line, as in line 3, the regularity constitutes an organic, expressive registration of the monotony of the spectacle:

Frŏm thénce/ă léngth/ŏf búrn/ĭng sánd/ăppéars./

Although there is much more wrong with the "Inebriety" passage than its meter, and much more right with the "Village" passage than metrical analysis alone can locate, it is clear that an organic meter does constitute one important signal of total poetic merit.

It is undoubtedly largely for metrical reasons that we turn with disappointment if not with loathing from Whitman's "O Captain! My Captain!", which, in its inexpressive stressing, is worthy of no one so much as Longfellow:

O Captain! my Captain! our fearful trip is done,
The ship has weather'd every rack, the prize we sought is won,
The port is near, the bells I hear, the people all exulting,
While follow eyes the steady keel, the vessel grim and daring.

The meter is as unnatural to Whitman's genius as the clumsy-genteel syntax ("While follow eyes the steady keel") and the dull diction (*fearful, people, exulting*). When we turn from such an exhibit to the work of the more genuine Whitman, we find that beneath the witty guise of free verse reside the same sort of expressive cadences that vivify verse composed expressively in more overtly traditional meters. Look, for example, at the beginning of Section 32 of *Song of Myself:*

I think I could turn and live with animals, they are so placid and
     self-contain'd,
I stand and look at them long and long.

Underlying these lines is a traditional framework of an iambic pentameter line followed by two iambic tetrameters, all exquisitely varied from the iambic base to reinforce the sense:

Ĭ thínk/Ĭ cŏuld túrn/ănd lĭve/wĭth án/ĭmăls,/

thĕy ăre/sŏ plá/cĭd ănd sélf/-cŏntáin'd,/

Ĭ stánd/ănd lóok/ăt thĕm lóng/ănd lóng./

When we scan and analyze, we perceive the use of the anapest in line 1 to enact the "turn," as well as the return to regularity in line 3—after the little skip of time embodied in the two unstressed syllables (*at them*) —as a realization of the simplicity and quiet of the new actions (standing and looking) which follow from the activity of the old (thinking). We could say that the poet who accomplishes such lines is a wholly different poet from the one who composed "O Captain!," and it is metrical analysis that helps us perceive the difference.

As we have seen, triple meters, as in "Annabel Lee," and fourteeners, as in "O Captain!," offer strong temptations to metrical inertness, although the historical pre-eminence of the iambic pentameter also leads to that meter's excessive domination over the poet whose rhythmical sense has not yet developed a sufficient resistance to imposed patterns. Tetrameter couplets threaten a similar danger, and only a master can use them without risking boredom. The mid-eighteenth-century poet Joseph Warton is not such a master, as his practice in the ode "To Fancy" indicates:

> Then guide me from this horrid scene
> To high-arched walks and alleys green,
> Where lovely Laura walks, to shun
> The fervours of the mid-day sun;
> The pangs of absence, O remove,
> For thou canst place me near my love,
> Canst fold in visionary bliss,
> And let me think I steal a kiss.

As we can see from this example, the difficulty of the iambic tetrameter couplet lies in the relative shortness of the lines: by the time the poet gets a base properly established in each line, he has run out of feet where substitutions might occur. The practice of Swift, in contrast, helps show how a general instinct for avoiding the tedious can overcome even the natural limitations of this verse form. Here is Swift in his "Epistle to a Lady

Who Desired the Author to Make Verses on Her in the Heroick Stile":

> . . . as
>
> It is well observ'd by Horace,
> Ridicule has greater Pow'r
> To reform the World, than Sour.
> Horses thus, let Jockeys judge else,
> Switches better guide than Cudgels.
> Bastings heavy, dry, obtuse,
> Only Dulness can produce,
> While a little gentle Jerking
> Sets the Spirits all a working.

Here Swift plays in and out of his metrical norm, surprising and delighting us by turns. Yeats is another who, taking a lesson from Swift, manages the tetrameter couplet with a masterful flexibility. His "Why Should Not Old Men Be Mad?," which we have met before, stands at the opposite metrical extreme from Warton's "To Fancy" because Yeats brings to bear the taste required to avoid the pitfall of regularity:

> Why should not old men be mad?
> Some have known a likely lad
> That had a sound fly-fisher's wrist
> Turn to a drunken journalist;
> A girl that knew all Dante once
> Live to bear children to a dunce.

Hardly a regular line at all here, and yet the variations are conducted with such tact that we are never permitted to forget the pattern of the basic meter that underlies the texture. The variations are managed not merely with a fine colloquial illusion but also with a highly formal sense of balance: for example, against the four-stress base, the first line—with its five stresses—gives an effect of excessive weight which may suggest imbalance; but the balance is restored in line 4, which offers now three instead of the expected four stresses. And line 3,

> Thăt hăd/ă sóund/ flý-físh/ĕr's wríst,/

balances its initial pyrrhic against a spondee in the third position so that, although an illusion of flexible colloquial utterance is transmitted, the illusion is not bought at the cost of any lessening of formality.

In metrical criticism the important principle to keep in mind is that the poet creates whole poems rather than the elements of poems: it is not his work to present "beautiful rhythms" but beautiful—that is, wholly coherent—poems (sometimes made out of very ugly subject matter) in which the rhythms perfectly fuse with the many other sources of meaning. Throughout the history of English poetry one poet after another has been elevated—temporarily, it always appears—as "a great creator of beautiful rhythms"; but if we adhere to the organic conception of a poem, we will reject this simpleminded kind of metrical criticism. An example is Max Beerbohm's response to the talents of Swinburne. As a young man, says Beerbohm, Swinburne resembled "a legendary creature, sole kin to the phoenix." "It had been impossible," Beerbohm once thought, "that he should ever surpass himself in the artistry that was from the outset his; impossible that he should bring forth rhythms lovelier and greater than those early rhythms, or exercise over them a mastery more than—absolute." If a poet were, like a drummer, a man who makes rhythms, this would be very well: but a poet is under the obligation of making poems, and no other activity from him will do. We now see that, for all his beautiful rhythms, Swinburne won't do because he has written no poems, that is, constructions of sufficient density and unity to call us back to them again and again. In arriving at this perception, we should humbly ask for the aesthetic wisdom to avoid Beerbohmism ourselves, to avoid overpraising contemporary poets for their command of one or another of the separate elements of their art.

Returning now to our axiom of economy and coherence, we can deduce a second critical principle: substitutions should be such as to participate in the total meaning, which is to say that they should be meaningful in themselves rather than accidental. As Aristotle says, speaking of the causal interconnection of the tragic episodes which produce a tragic action, "A thing whose presence or absence makes no visible difference, is not an organic part of the whole." Every work of art, as Aristotle finds in another place, must carry within itself a demonstration of the reason why its shape is as it is and not otherwise. Ideally, then, every substitution or variation from the metrical norm in a poem should justify itself by the sanction of meaning: nothing should happen metrically without a reason deriving from the significance of the total poem. We have to insist, however, on the qualification "ideally": no work of art is perfect—it would probably kill us if it were—and we finally learn to appraise poetic technique by its mere approaches to the ideal of perfection.

We have seen that initial dissyllabic substitution for the sake of variety alone is a usage sanctioned by convention and perhaps necessitated by circumstance. But a medial substitution has no such sanction: every medial substitution ought to have the power to persuade us that, given the local pressures of emotion and utterance, it is entirely inevitable. Meaningless medial substitution, which reverses the rhythm and gives the reader either a jolt (if trochaic) or a steady push (if spondaic), is a common sign of metrical ineptitude, and one—it is sad to have to say it—which characterizes a great deal of contemporary poetry and almost-contemporary poetry. It would be hard to specify, for example, the function of the variations in these lines from a sonnet of John Masefield's:

> Is there a great green commonwealth of Thought
> Which ranks the yearly pageant, and decides
> How Summer's royal progress shall be wrought,
> By secret stir which in each plant abides?

Or in these, from George Barker's "Memorial":

> The seagull, spreadeagled, splayed on the wind,
> Span backwards shrieking, belly facing upward,
> Fled backwards with a gimlet in its heart
> To see the two youths swimming hand in hand
> Through green eternity. O swept overboard
> Nor could the thirty-foot jaws them part. . . .

Richard Wilbur, on the other hand, demonstrates his accuracy and tact as a metrist in "A Simile for Her Smile," where almost every variation convinces us that it issues from the pressure of the poem's internal dynamics:

> Your smiling, or the hope, the thought of it,
> Mákes ĭn/my mind such pause and ab/rúpt éase/
> As when the highway bridgegates fall,
> Bálkĭng/the hasty traffic. . . .

Here even the initial trochees in lines 2 and 4, which might easily be justified conventionally by the necessity of mere rhythmical relief after the strings of preceding iambic feet, undertake a distinct and precise role in the expression: each signals the surprising advent of an action. And the other substitution, the terminal spondee in line 2, realizes perfectly the abruptness of sudden refreshment after heat, haste, and noise. All this is not to say that Wilbur is a better poet than Masefield or Barker: it is only to say that he is a better metrist, and thus perhaps stands a better chance of producing something ultimately which will exploit simultaneously all the resources of language rather than merely some of them. He reveals that he knows what density of texture is, and he reveals a mastery of one of the main techniques for attaining it, the interfusion of predication and rhythm.

The lust for rhythm is so universal in readers of poetry that a poet can hardly be said to have a choice about whether his poem shall be rhythmical or not: his only choice is whether he is going to use meter well or ill, efficiently or inefficiently. If he tries to write "without" meter, it is certain that his readers are going to restore meter to his poem, and, in the process, as I. A. Richards has shown in *Practical Criticism*, misread it. Attempts to "escape" from meter—or at least some kind of governing rhythm—are thus almost equivalent to attempts to escape from poetry. In lines so metrically meaningless as these, from Josephine Jacobsen's "For Any Member of the Security Police," we feel that one dimension is simply missing:

> Let us ask you a few questions, without rancor,
> In simple curiosity, putting aside
> Our reactions or the rising of our gorge,
> As a child asks, How does it work? As premise:
>
> Some limitations you admit: soundproofing
> Is never perfect, hints rise from any cellar;
> There are a few—a very few—for whom reshaping
> Must be abandoned for that catchall, death. . . .

Here the price paid for the neglect of the metrical dimension is severe, and it is a price exacted from a great many contemporary poets whose devotion to politics and revolutions, personal and social, transcends their devotion to the art of poetry.

Many contemporary American poets have been tempted to renounce rhythm on the grounds that, associated as it is with the traditional usages of England and the Continent, it is somehow un-American. And it is probably true that the special tonalities of American idiom do require some adjustments in traditional prosodic usages. Robert Frost is one who has perceived that American idiom calls for special metrical treatment, but in working out that treatment he has adapted the proven expressive resources of English prosody. The poet E. L. Mayo has appraised Frost's achievement in embodying metrically the unique tone of the American language. He writes:

Effective meter is closely bound up with the matter of living idiom. . . . Frost's line from "Birches,"

> Kícking his wáy dówn through the áir to the gróund,

never fails to give me pleasure because it accommodates itself so well to the purpose it serves in the poem (sudden activity after inhibited movement) without violating American speech idiom at any point. Some of the most casual and common idioms of the language have strongly developed metrical elements; for example:

> Í tóld hǐm hálf ǎ dózěn tímes
> Whéthěr yǒu líke ǐt ǒr nót
> Ís thěre ánȳ réal réasǒn whȳ yǒu cán't?

(the list might be endlessly prolonged) and I conceive it the duty of the poet who desires authenticity of sound and movement to cultivate his ear, avail himself of these riches that lie so close to hand whenever they serve his purpose. In this way his metrical effects become more than merely personal; they become *native*. He thus clothes his naked uniqueness (no fear—it will be civilized and intensified, not smothered by the clothing) in the real spoken language of the time.

And we can add that Frost not only registers the rhythms of "the real spoken language of the time"—not perhaps the real work of poetry: consider Milton and Keats—but more importantly manages to subsume these rhythms within the inherited meters of English. What he does is to fuse the living language with the metrical inheritance, and what he produces thereby is an illusion of faultless authenticity, a way with rhythm which owes a complex allegiance at once to past and present.

Frost's sense of the "meter-making argument" is one of the most memorable things about his whole art. A poem like "The Vantage Point" gives us a sample of his metrical skill:

> If tired of trees I seek again mankind,
>> Well I know where to hie me—in the dawn,
>> To a slope where the cattle keep the lawn.
> There amid lolling juniper reclined,
> Myself unseen, I see in white defined
>> Far off the homes of men, and farther still,
>> The graves of men on an opposing hill,
> Living or dead, whichever are to mind.
>
> And if by noon I have too much of these,
>> I have but to turn on my arm, and lo,
>> The sunburned hillside sets my face aglow,
> My breathing shakes the bluet like a breeze,
>> I smell the earth, I smell the bruisèd plant,
>> I look into the crater of the ant.

This is a poem of large contrasts and oppositions: distance and nearness, abstract and concrete, man and nature, reasonableness and sensuousness, even morning and afternoon. If the atmosphere of the first eight lines is one of reasonable detachment, that of the final six is one of devoted, physical, and even muscular commitment, and that is where the irony lies, since the two parts pretend to a choice between quite equal alternatives. The technical problem for the poet is how to manage the transition from the one atmosphere to the other, and, furthermore, how to enlist the reader's fullest participation in this crucial transition.

Frost solves this technical problem largely through meter. The first eight lines establish an informally varied iambic pentameter norm against which meaningful variation can occur. Everything proceeds normally and calmly until line 10, which is the pivot of the poem, the "turn" both thematically, structurally, and metrically. Line 9 introduces the metrical crux which is to follow by enforcing a background of vigorous iambic regularity with only one variation:

Ănd íf/bў nóon/Ĭ háve/tóo múch/ŏf thése./

The reader has now been fully prepared to participate almost bodily with the speaker in the "turn":

Ĭ háve/bŭt tŏ/túrn ŏn/mў árm,/ănd ló./

The medial trochee constitutes the thematic center of the poem as well as the metrical pivot: it forces us almost physically to turn in concert with the speaker, to participate not merely emotionally and intellectually in his predications but bodily as well in his very muscular movement. It forces us to participate fully, with head and heart, and with arms and shoulders. We wonder the more at Frost's technical achievement here when we realize that the effect of a triple rhythm is merely an illusion: no trisyllabic substitution has in fact taken place—the line is a strict decasyllable in harmony with all the other lines. With merely two restrained dissyllabic substitutions—a pyrrhic and a trochee—Frost has executed his effect with impressive control and economy. Not a syllable is wasted. And we can understand something about metrical traditions, about the way certain effects enter literary history and assume almost a life of their own, by recalling Whitman's similar metrical treatment of an act of physical and bodily "turning":

Ĭ thínk/Ĭ cŏuld túrn/ănd líve/wĭth án/ĭmăls/. . . .

Frost's effect is bolder than Whitman's, but the act they are executing, both physically and metrically, and the philosophic motivations of that act, ally them technically as well as thematically.

"The Vantage Point" is a poem whose fullest meaning is revealed to us by the substitution of two metrical feet. William Blake's "The Sick Rose" is perhaps an even more impressive metrical achievement, for the whole poem depends upon one crucial substitution. Here the base against which the substitution has power to operate is iambic-anapestic:

> O Rose, thou art sick!
> The invisible worm
> That flies in the night,
> In the howling storm
>
> Has found out thy bed
> Of crimson joy,
> And his dark secret love
> Does thy life destroy.

All goes swimmingly until line 7. Until we arrive there, the meter has kept us in the world of some possibility, a world in which escape is thinkable and in which even salvation may be engineered. If we have been shown an invisible worm flying in the night, if we have experienced a howling storm, we have also been conducted to a bed of a compensating crimson joy. But after line 7, hope is no longer possible, and the cause that extinguishes hope is a spondaic substitution, the only one in the poem:

Ănd hĭs/dárk séc/rĕt lóve/

It is this line that consummates the love, and it is this central spondaic foot that is the metrical consummation of the whole structure. The meter conducts the argument. The meter is the poem.

The art of poetry is the art of knowing language and people equally well. It is an art whose focus is in two directions at once: toward the inert technical arcana of syllables and sounds and syntax and metaphor as well as toward the animated actualities of human nature and human expectation. The knowledge of the way the reader will react when a technical something is done to him is what controls the poet's manipulation of his technique. To do something to the reader is the end of poetry: a poem is less a notation on a page or a sequence of uttered sounds than a shaped and measured formal effect that impinges upon a reader or hearer. The reality of the poem is in its impingement. As we saw at the outset, no element of a poem is more basic—and I mean physical—in its effect upon the reader than the metrical element, and perhaps no technical triumphs reveal more readily than the metrical the poet's sympathy with that universal human nature—conceived as a system of physiological and psychological uniformity—which exists outside his own, and to which the fullest understanding of his own is the key. The poet whose metrical effects actually work upon a reader reveals that he has attained an understanding of what man in general is like. It is thus possible to suggest that a great metrical achievement is more than the mark of a good technician: it is something like the signature of a great man.

PART TWO

Poetic Form

7

Structural Principles:
The Example of the Sonnet

In *The New Criticism*, John Crowe Ransom set forth a useful distinction between the texture and the structure of a poem. The texture, he found, is "local," unique to a given poem, while the structure involves the larger elements of form which ally the poem with a tradition or with history or with a wider world of recurring shapes. So far we have been considering one element, the metrical, which makes a contribution to poetic texture. We are now going to examine something quite different, poetic structure, which will oblige us to inquire into the nature of the organization and patterning of whole poetic lines and line groups which, by their special arrangements, express the kind of order that dominates in a given poem.

Regarded in the most general way, any poem exhibits one of two kinds of basic organization: it is either stichic or strophic. In stichic organization, line follows line without any formal or mathematical grouping of the lines into stanzas; in strophic organization, the lines are arranged in stanzas of varying degrees of logical complexity. *Paradise Lost* is a stichic poem; *The Faerie Queene* is strophic. In addition to these two fundamental sorts of poetic organization, we have also the kind of compromise between them represented by a poem written in, say, heroic couplets: such couplets can be called stanzas only by courtesy. They could more accurately be called something like additive units, and perhaps a poem in heroic couplets is best thought of as essentially stichic, with a "line" of twenty rather than of ten syllables.

Stichic organization has been found most appropriate for large, expansive narrative, dramatic, and meditative actions: *Paradise Lost, King Lear, The Prelude, Four Quartets* are stichic. Strophic organization, on the other hand, has been found most appropriate for dense and closely circumscribed moments of emotion or argument. Since strophic structure is associated with music—the codas and repeats of music are analogous to the rhymes and refrains of lyric strophes—we expect the materials which normally find their way into songs likewise to find their way into poetic strophes: we expect moments of celebration or reminiscence to shape themselves into strophes, while we expect social commentary or depictions of social or ethical action to seek stichic form.

The essential element of coherence in a strophe, or stanza, is end-rhyme, although lines can be organized into stanzas without it. Rhyme is a much more complicated matter than it appears to be, for it often involves not merely the sound relationships which it advertises so blatantly but, surprisingly, important logical and semantic relationships as well. W. K. Wimsatt, in his essay "One Relation of Rhyme to Reason," has emphasized that every rhyme invites the reader's consideration of semantic as well as of sound similarities. A good example of this logical dimension often present in rhyme is a stanza from Pound's *Mauberley,* where we find the speaker at pains to contrast two kinds of art, the commercial-facile and the permanent:

> The 'age demanded' chiefly a mould in plaster,
> Made with no loss of time.
> A prose kinema, not, not assuredly, alabaster
> Or the 'sculpture' of rhyme.

Here *plaster* and *alabaster* "sound alike," all right, just as *time* and *rhyme* do. But when we inquire why they have been disposed so that their sound resemblances will organize the stanza, we perceive that their relationships are not only logical but witty as well. Plaster and alabaster are total opposites as materials for plastic art: plaster is squeezed or molded into some predetermined shape; it often apes some other material—most often stone—and it is conspicuously fragile and impermanent. Alabaster, on the other hand, must be worked from the outside: it must be incised, and incision implies a sharpness in both the cutting tool and the intelligence that commands it. The shape of a figure cut in alabaster cannot be wholly predetermined, for it will depend in part on the unique texture of the stone. And finally, no one works in alabaster without some aspirations toward permanence.

By rhyming the words which represent these two rich symbols of technical, aesthetic opposition, the stanza appears to compare them, while ironically it actually contrasts them. That is, the sound similarity "says" that they resemble each other, while the rhetoric of the stanza asserts their difference. We are moved in two directions at once, or we are abused only to be disabused: irony is the result. A similar sort of irony results from the rhyming of *time* and *rhyme*—or actually of *no loss of time* with *'sculpture' of rhyme*. The sound similarity implies a semantic similarity between fast manufacturing and permanent beauty. And again, our perception that the implied comparison is really masking a significant contrast produces our experience of irony. Wimsatt's demonstration focuses largely on the brilliant rhyme usages of Alexander Pope, but once we have understood the kinds of semantic meaning that rhymes imply we can find examples in all periods of English poetry.

We can find examples in our most instinctive colloquial phrasings as well, many of which suggest that we all operate in accord with an impulse to make language artistic. We say that someone *beats* a hasty *retreat* instead of leaves rapidly because we want words to show their music. The British speak of a *sticky wicket*. Americans own their houses *free* and *clear* and like to descant knowingly about the *name* of the *game*. If not too blatant, rhyme in conversation surprises and gratifies us. Poems exploit our pleasure in this kind of harmony by organizing these pleasant sound similarities into elaborate formal structures. The Chinese student quoted by Pound as saying that "Poetry consists of *gists* and *piths*" we remember because in his remark he has approximated poetry by rhyming, or at least by paying his dues to the artistic principle of assonance. In the same way, clichés become clichés because they resemble poetry: *to have and to hold* binds the two ideas through an alliteration that says something more than the words say. Although our age seems to have lost the sense that rhyme betokens "accord," in the Renaissance the idea was a rich commonplace, with impressive erotic advantage to writers like Spenser, whose *Epithalamion,* a poem celebrating his own marriage, is also a poem celebrating his own rhymes. And there is the following, written by we don't know whom four hundred years ago, which time has been unwilling to let die—because of what it says, of course, but also because of its rhyme, and not merely its end-rhyme:

> There is a lady sweet and kind,
> Was never face so pleased my mind.

The technical problems facing the poet are very different in stichic and in strophic organization. The poet writing in stichic form—at least since the demise of Old English prosody—must make decisions constantly about enjambment, or run-on lines. As he composes each line he must decide whether it should remain as a distinct unit—should exhibit line integrity—or whether it should run on to the beginning of the next line and fuse its syntax and its rhythms with it. If a stichic poem exhibits line integrity, the effect will resemble mosaic: we will get a sense of a whole constructed of tiny parts of roughly the same size and weight. But if a stichic poem exhibits a high degree of enjambment, we get quite a different sense: we get a symphonic sense of flow and flux, a sort of tidal variation. Consider the difference in structure between the verse of Thomson's "Winter":

> To thee, the patron of this first essay,
> The Muse, O Wilmington! renews her song.
> Since she has rounded the revolving year:
> Skimmed the gay Spring; on eagle-pinions borne,
> Attempted through the Summer-blaze to rise;

> Then swept o'er Autumn with the shadowy gale;
> And now among the Wintry clouds again,
> Rolled in the doubling storm, she tries to soar,
> To swell her note with all the rushing winds,
> To suit her swelling cadence to the floods.

and that of *Paradise Lost:*

> Only begotten Son, seest thou what rage
> Transports our adversary, whom no bounds
> Prescrib'd, no bars of Hell, nor all the chains
> Heapt on him there, nor yet the main Abyss
> Wide interrupt can hold; so bent he seems
> On desperate revenge, that shall redound
> Upon his own rebellious head. . . .

Both passages are in "blank verse," but that term goes only a very little way in describing them. The technique of the Thomson passage is very close to that of the end-stopped heroic couplet: we are moved forward by line units and almost by syntactical units of predictable length and weight, and the effect is one of closure, of taking up a thing only when the thing preceding it is entirely finished. The view is analytic: the materials are being accumulated, like mosaic, piece by piece. But in the Milton passage the enjambment helps transmit a very different effect, an effect of strenuousness, of an energy that disdains containment, bursting through the line endings as if they constituted impious bars to liberty.

In the same way, the term "heroic couplet" does not describe anything very precisely unless we indicate also whether the couplets are end-stopped or run-on. Despite very occasional enjambment, as in "The Rape of the Lock,"

> This Nymph, to the destruction of mankind,
> Nourished two Locks, which graceful hung behind
> In equal curls, and well conspired to deck
> With shining ringlets the smooth iv'ry neck,

Pope customarily end-stops tightly, and his end-stopping helps register his customary analytic view of his materials:

> To plant, to build, whatever you intend,
> To rear the Column, or the Arch to bend,
> To swell the Terrace, or to sink the Grot;
> In all, let Nature never be forgot.
> But treat the Goddess like a modest fair,
> Nor over-dress, nor leave her wholly bare.

The "heroic couplets" of Keats, on the other hand, bear very little resemblance to Pope's, or to Chaucer's, or to Dryden's: notice the boldness of enjambment in "Endymion":

> Full in the middle of this pleasantness
> There stood a marble altar, with a tress
> Of flowers budded newly; and the dew
> Had taken fairy phantasies to strew
> Daisies upon the sacred sward last eve. . . .

More consequential ultimately than the difference between a loose stichic form like blank verse and a tight one like the couplet is the degree of enjambment. It is commonly thought that blank verse is a more informal mode than the heroic couplet, but in his *Irene,* Samuel Johnson writes end-stopped blank verse lines which generate a much more formal atmosphere than the run-on rhymed couplets of Keats.

The decisions a poet makes about enjambment, whether he is rhyming or not, will tend to imply his sense of relation to inherited stichic tradition, for the tradition in stichic poetry is that of a high degree of line integrity. By his particular strategy of enjambment, consequently, the poet takes a stance toward a tradition as well as expressing an attitude toward the amount of flux he feels appropriate to the treatment he brings to his subject.

If the degree of significant line integrity is one of the main formal concerns of the stichic poet, the problems facing the strophic poet are much more taxing. One of the most ubiquitous of English fixed forms, the sonnet, with its elaborate scheme of rhyme and logical relationships, provides good examples of some of the universal problems of strophic form.

The sonnet is a fourteen-line poem in iambic pentameter: the rhyme scheme and the mode of logical organization implied by it determine the type. The most common type is the Petrarchan or Italian sonnet, which rhymes like this:

$$
\text{OCTAVE}
\begin{cases}
\left.\begin{array}{l} a \\ b \\ b \\ a \end{array}\right\} \text{FIRST QUATRAIN} \\[1em]
\left.\begin{array}{l} a \\ b \\ b \\ a \end{array}\right\} \text{SECOND QUATRAIN}
\end{cases}
$$

TURN $\longrightarrow$

$$
\text{SESTET}
\begin{cases}
c \\ d \\ c \\ d \\ c \\ d
\end{cases}
$$

The rhyme scheme of the sestet is variable: sometimes it takes the form *cdecde,* or *cdeced,* or *cdcdee.* Structurally, the Petrarchan sonnet consists of three parts (two quatrains and the sestet) which underlie an unbalanced bipartite shape (octave and sestet). The sonnet's structural identity lies in just this imbalance: the first eight lines constitute a weightier quantitative unit than the last six: if the two parts of the sonnet were equal in number of lines, the form would risk the dullness of perfect symmetry—of a painting whose main effect occurs exactly in the center, for example, or of a line unrelieved by any hint of crookedness or deviation from geometrical exactitude. The poet who understands the sonnet form is the one who has developed an instinct for exploiting the principle of imbalance. And to emphasize the distinction between octave and sestet, the poet tries to make the rhyme-words of the final six lines as different as possible from those of the preceding eight. Hopkins expresses the principle pleasantly: "When one goes so far as to run the rhymes of the octave into the sestet a downright prolapsus or hernia takes place and the sonnet is crippled for life."

A characteristic of the Petrarchan sonnet is its convention of the "turn," which normally occurs at the start of line 9, the beginning of the sestet. It is perhaps more accurate to say that the turn occurs somewhere in the white space that separates line 8 from line 9, and that line 9 simply reflects or records it. But wherever we think of it as actually taking place, something very important, something indeed indispensable to the action of the Petrarchan sonnet, happens at the turn: we are presented there with a logical or emotional shift by which the speaker enables himself to take a new or altered or enlarged view of his subject.

The standard way of constructing a Petrarchan sonnet is to project the subject in the first quatrain; to develop or complicate it in the second; then to execute, at the beginning of the sestet, the turn which will open up for solution the problem advanced by the octave, or which will ease the load of idea or emotion borne by the octave, or which will release the pressure accumulated in the octave. The octave and the sestet conduct actions which are analogous to the actions of inhaling and exhaling, or of contraction and release in the muscular system. The one builds up the pressure, the other releases it; and the turn is the dramatic and climactic center of the poem, the place where the intellectual or emotional method of release first becomes clear and possible. From line 9 it is usually plain sailing down to the end of the sestet and the resolution of the experience. If the two parts of the sonnet, although quantitatively unequal, can be said to resemble the two sides of an equation, then the turn is something like the equals sign: it sets into action the relationship between two things, and triggers a total statement. We may even suggest that one of the emotional archetypes of the Petrarchan sonnet structure is the pattern of sexual pressure and release. Surely no sonnet succeeds as a sonnet that does not execute at the turn something analogous to the general kinds of "release" with which the reader's muscles and nervous system are familiar.

George Santayana's "As in the Midst of Battle" is a good representative Petrarchan sonnet in which the turn is particularly conspicuous:

> As in the midst of battle there is room
> For thoughts of love, and in foul sin for mirth;
> As gossips whisper of a trinket's worth
> Spied by the death-bed's flickering candle-gloom;
> As in the crevices of Caesar's tomb
> The sweet herbs flourish on a little earth:
> So in this great disaster of our birth
> We can be happy, and forget our doom.

> For morning, with a ray of tenderest joy
> Gilding the iron heaven, hides the truth,
> And evening gently woos us to employ
> Our grief in idle catches. Such is youth;
> Till from that summer's trance we wake, to find
> Despair before us, vanity behind.

Here the turn, which we can designate as represented by the one word *For,* is a logical action: it initiates an answer to the question posed implicitly by the octave: "How on earth can we be happy when we know that we are doomed?" On the other hand, the turn in Keats's "On First Looking into Chapman's Homer" is less a moment of logical intensity than a moment of sheer metaphoric power, of an energetic breakthrough into a new figurative world. Santayana's turn is manifested in *For;* Keats's in *Then felt I like:*

> Much have I travell'd in the realms of gold,
> And many goodly states and kingdoms seen;
> Round many western islands have I been
> Which bards in fealty to Apollo hold.
> Oft of one wide expanse had I been told
> That deep-brow'd Homer ruled as his demesne;
> Yet did I never breathe its pure serene
> Till I heard Chapman speak out loud and bold:
>
> Then felt I like some watcher of the skies
> When a new planet swims into his ken;
> Or like stout Cortez when with eagle eyes
> He star'd at the Pacific—and all his men
> Look'd at each other with a wild surmise—
> Silent, upon a peak in Darien.

This turn admits us into a new kind of imagery: we pass at line 9 from the octave's images of real-estate and worldly principalities and well-conducted travel to the sestet's infinitely more exciting images of discovery, both of a new planet and of a whole new ocean. The turn releases us from the element of earth, and we enter the elements of air and water, elements which achieve a special union here because of the metaphor by which the new planet "swims."

Sometimes the turn signals a shift in address or rhetorical focus,

as it does in Wordsworth's "It Is a Beauteous Evening," where the
octave establishes the relation between the speaker and the setting
and where the sestet answers the question implicit in that relation: "Why am I so moved by this scene, and why is my daughter
not moved likewise?" The rhetorical turn here is almost like that
in Frost's "The Vantage Point" in that it coincides wittily with
something like a literal turn of the body or the head:

> It is a beauteous evening, calm and free,
> The holy time is quiet as a Nun
> Breathless with adoration; the broad sun
> Is sinking down in its tranquillity;
> The gentleness of heaven broods o'er the Sea:
> Listen! the mighty Being is awake,
> And doth with his eternal motion make
> A sound like thunder—everlastingly.
>
> Dear Child! dear Girl; that walkest with me here,
> If thou appear untouched by solemn thought,
> Thy nature is not therefore less divine:
> Thou liest in Abraham's bosom all the year;
> And worshipp'st at the temple's inner shrine,
> God being with thee when we know it not.

And sometimes the turn is an occasion for springing a naughty
surprise, as in this sonnet by J. K. Stephen:

> Two voices are there: one is of the deep;
> It learns the storm-cloud's thunderous melody,
> Now roars, now murmurs with the changing sea,
> Now bird-like pipes, now closes soft in sleep:
> And one is of an old half-witted sheep
> Which bleats articulate monotony,
> And indicates that two and one are three,
> That grass is green, lakes damp, and mountains steep:
>
> And, Wordsworth, both are thine: at certain times
> Forth from the heart of thy melodious rhymes
> The form and pressure of high thoughts will burst:
> At other times—good Lord! I'd rather be
> Quite unacquainted with the A. B. C.
> Than write such hopeless rubbish as thy worst.

This poem works its witty purpose so successfully in part because it is technically such a perfect sonnet. The assignment of the two quatrains of the octave to the treatment of the two "voices" constitutes a nice adaptation of matter to form, and the use of the sestet rhymes to relate ideas logically and ironically is admirable (consider, for example, the ironic relation between *burst* and *worst*). Part of the fun resides in this very technical perfection, lavished as it is on a fairly "low" enterprise. For the contemporary reader, part of the fun also arose from specific verbal parody: Stephen's line 12, for example, neatly recalls the turn of Wordsworth's own sonnet "The World Is Too Much with Us," whose sestet begins:

> It moves us not.—Great God! I'd rather be
> A Pagan suckled in a creed outworn. . . .

Writing a good Petrarchan sonnet is difficult; writing a superb one is all but impossible. So demanding is the form that only the very greatest masters have managed to avoid its two main technical pitfalls. The first is what we can call a lack of appropriate density in the octave. There is always the temptation in the second quatrain merely to repeat or to reproject the matter of the first instead of advancing or really complicating the argument, description, or emotion. The sestet is usually sufficiently dense and tight, for it has a distinct job of reconciling or solving or unraveling to perform, and in relatively short compass: the problem lies in packing the octave with similarly tight and complex materials. It is the second quatrain that poses a challenge to every poet's capacity for genuine—rather than merely apparent—thematic development. The second technical difficulty in the Petrarchan sonnet is connected with the "envelope" rhyme scheme of the two quatrains. By envelope we mean that the two "outside" rhymes (the *a*'s) serve as an envelope or container of the internal couplet (the *b*'s). Because of their logical as well as their sound relationships, ideally the phrases or clauses rhymed *a* should relate closely to each other, even though they are separated; and those within the envelope, those which comprise the couplet rhymed *b*, should exhibit an even closer semantic and logical relationship. The general critical principle, which follows from the axiom that a poem is organic and that everything in it must contribute to meaning, is that the rhyming of two contiguous lines demands a tighter logical unity between them than between two noncontiguous lines which rhyme. We expect the relation of the two lines of a couplet to be logically very close, whereas the relation of two rhyming lines in an *abab* quatrain does not arouse such rigorous expectations. The approximation of structures of reasoning to the shape of the rhyme scheme is one of the most difficult acts in English poetry: indeed, only a few masters of the sonnet in English have managed always to avoid meaningless rhyming.

One variation on the Petrarchan form is the so-called Miltonic sonnet, in which we encounter the turn not at the beginning of line 9 but within it, or even later:

> When I consider how my light is spent,
> Ere half my days, in this dark world and wide,
> And that one Talent which is death to hide
> Lodg'd with me useless, though my Soul more bent
> To serve therewith my Maker, and present
> My true account, lest he returning chide;
> Doth God exact day-labour, light denied,
> I fondly ask; But patience to prevent
>
> That murmur, soon replies, God doth not need
> Either man's work or his own gifts; who best
> Bear his mild yoke, they serve him best; his State
> Is Kingly. Thousands at his bidding speed
> And post o'er Land and Ocean without rest:
> They also serve who only stand and wait.

It would seem that Milton's urge to vary the position of the turn is a part of his larger tendency toward emotional enjambment: there is always something in fixed forms that stimulates Milton to mild rebellion or exhibitions of technical independence. That Robert Frost shares these qualities seems apparent from his practice in "The Vantage Point," which is a good modern example of the Miltonic delay in enacting the turn.

A different rhyme scheme and thus a different convention of logical and rhetorical organization governs the Shakespearean or English sonnet. Here, instead of a basic structure of two parts laid over three, we find a structure of two parts laid over four.

The two parts are the three quatrains, on the one hand, and the concluding or resolving couplet, on the other. The abstract shape looks like this:

$$
\left.
\begin{array}{l}
a \\
b \\
a \\
b
\end{array}
\right\} \text{FIRST QUATRAIN}
$$

$$
\left.
\begin{array}{l}
c \\
d \\
c \\
d
\end{array}
\right\} \text{SECOND QUATRAIN}
$$

$$
\left.
\begin{array}{l}
e \\
f \\
e \\
f
\end{array}
\right\} \text{THIRD QUATRAIN}
$$

TURN⟶

$$
\left.
\begin{array}{l}
g \\
g
\end{array}
\right\} \text{COUPLET}
$$

The turn normally occurs at the beginning of line 13, although the force of the earlier Petrarchan convention is such that it occasionally visits the Shakespearean form and leaves its mark as a slight turn at the beginning of the third quatrain or somewhere within it. If the Petrarchan form poses a problem in the dense and organic development of the second quatrain, the Shakespearean form asks even more of the poet's capacity to develop rather than merely to repeat or to vary or to embellish, for ideally each of the quatrains should serve in its own way to complicate the situation or to advance the dilemma which it is the couplet's business to resolve. Shakespeare's "Sonnet XXIX" illustrates not only the relation of the first twelve lines to the concluding couplet but also, by the turns at the beginning of line 9 and in the middle of line 10, the force of the tradition of Petrarchan structure:

> When in disgrace with fortune and men's eyes
> I all alone beweep my outcast state,
> And trouble deaf heaven with my bootless cries,
> And look upon myself, and curse my fate,
> Wishing me like to one more rich in hope,

> Featur'd like him, like him with friends possess'd,
> Desiring this man's art, and that man's scope,
> With what I most enjoy contented least:
> Yet in these thoughts myself almost despising,
> Haply I think on thee,—and then my state,
> Like to the lark at break of day arising
> From sullen earth, sings hymns at heaven's gate;
>
> For thy sweet love remember'd such wealth brings
> That then I scorn to change my state with kings.

Although the basic action of both Petrarchan and Shakespearean sonnets is similar, it is the proportioning that makes the immense difference between them. Both present and then "solve" problems, the Petrarchan form in its octave and sestet, the Shakespearean in its comparatively hypertrophied initial twelve lines and then in its couplet. In the Petrarchan sonnet the problem is often solved by reasoned perception or by a relatively expansive and formal meditative process, for the sestet allows enough room for the undertaking of prudent, highly reasonable kinds of resolutions. But in the Shakespearean sonnet, because resolution must take place within the tiny compass of a twenty-syllable couplet, the "solution" is more likely to be the fruit of wit, or paradox, or even a quick shaft of sophistry, logical cleverness, or outright comedy. In the Shakespearean sonnet the turn tends to pivot on one of the logical adverbs—*for, then, so, but, yet, lest, thus, therefore*—words which constitute syntactical figures of self-conscious dialectic. The crucial operations of such words in assisting the Shakespearean sonneteer to "solve his problem" tend to make the Shakespearean sonnet a little showplace of rhetoric or advocacy or logic—or mock-logic. Furthermore, the very disproportion of the two parts of the Shakespearean sonnet, the gross imbalance between the twelve-line problem and the two-line solution, has about it something vaguely risible and even straight-faced farcical: it invites images of balloons and pins.

And even when the final couplet does not resolve the conflicts or entanglements presented by the preceding quatrains, there remains something ineffably witty about the form of the Shakespearean sonnet, something that distinguishes it essentially as a form from the Petrarchan. If the shape of the Petrarchan sonnet, with its two slightly unbalanced sections devoted to pressure and release, seems to accord with the dynamics of much emotional experience, the shape of the Shakespearean, with its smaller units and its "commentary" couplet, seems to accord with the modes of the intellectual, analytic, and even satiric operations of the human sensibility. Shakespeare seems to imply as much, indeed, in his use of the English rather than the Petrarchan form in *Romeo and Juliet,* I, v, 95ff., where the two lovers find in the structure of the English sonnet the perfect vehicle for what is less an emotional experience than a mock-academic *débat.*

The Petrarchan and the Shakespearean are the most common sonnet forms in English. Edmund Spenser introduced another, but few poets have taken to it. The Spenserian sonnet is structured essentially like the Shakespearean: it consists of three quatrains and a final couplet. The difference is that the Spenserian form overlaps the rhymes at the junctions of the quatrains, thus:

$$
\begin{array}{l}
\left.\begin{array}{l} a \\ b \\ a \end{array}\right\} \text{FIRST QUATRAIN} \\
\text{INTERNAL COUPLET} \left\{\begin{array}{l} b \\ b \end{array}\right. \\
\left.\begin{array}{l} c \\ b \end{array}\right\} \text{SECOND QUATRAIN} \\
\text{INTERNAL COUPLET} \left\{\begin{array}{l} c \\ c \end{array}\right. \\
\left.\begin{array}{l} d \\ c \\ d \end{array}\right\} \text{THIRD QUATRAIN} \\
\left.\begin{array}{l} e \\ e \end{array}\right\} \text{COUPLET}
\end{array}
$$

The effect of the two internal couplets is to fuse the quatrains to each other and to provide a structural basis for a special tightness in the reasoning.

But in the following, from Spenser's *Amoretti,* we have an interesting example of a disturbing internal conflict between an essentially Shakespearean sound form and an essentially Petrarchan logical structure. The solution or release begins with the Petrarchan turn at line 9, and, despite the contrary suggestions of the rhyme scheme, the final couplet does not stand alone but extends itself as merely a further part of the sestet:

> One day I wrote her name upon the strand,
> But came the waves and washèd it away:
> Agayne I wrote it with a second hand,
> But came the tyde, and made my paynes his pray.
> Vayne man, sayd she, that doest in vaine assay
> A mortall thing so to immortalize!
> For I my selve shall lyke to this decay,
> And eek my name bee wypèd out lykewize.
> Not so (quod I) let baser things devize
> To dy in dust, but you shall live by fame:
> My verse your vertues rare shall eternize,
> And in the hevens wryte your glorious name;
>
> > Where, whenas death shall all the world subdew,
> > Our love shall live, and later life renew.

From the structural schizophrenia of this sonnet, from the internal warfare taking place between its abstract rhyme structure and its organization of thought, we can perceive two principles, one particular and one general. First, we see that the two basic sonnet forms, the Petrarchan and the Shakespearean, do not function similarly—indeed, that is why there are two of them. Their respective ways of organizing their elements through rhyme presuppose different operations of the mind and the emotions. To turn at line 9 and to resolve in six lines is a very different emotional operation than to turn at line 13 and to resolve in two. Secondly, we see from the opposition between form and matter in this sonnet of Spenser's the more general critical principle which underlies all stanzaic form: the principle of expressive form, or accommodation. That is, the sense and the form should adapt to each other: if a couplet follows a series of quatrains, the matter of the couplet should differ from the matter of the quatrains for the rhyme scheme to justify itself aesthetically and take its place as a fully expressive, organic element in the poem.

Given the universal psychological appeal of the sonnet structure of complication followed by resolution—an archetype of the common act of problem-solving, or deciding, or even rationalizing—numerous variations are inevitable, although few have won the sanction of custom. One that has not is Sir Philip Sidney's experiment, in *Astrophel and Stella,* with an English sonnet in hexameter rather than pentameter lines. Here Sidney seems to encounter the difficulty familiar to all poets who have tried to produce English hexameters in sequence, whether in stichic or strophic arrangements: the hexameter contains an even number of feet, and frequently an even number of stresses; it thus tends to break in the middle into two exactly even—hence monotonous —segments in a way that the pentameter, with its odd number of feet, does not. Nor has Shakespeare's analogous experiment with a sonnet in tetrameter instead of pentameter lines ("Sonnet cxlv") stimulated much imitation: now the rhymes seem to occur at excessively short intervals, and we get the illusion of being carried along too rapidly for the assertions to justify their importance.

A further variation of the sonnet form has been promulgated by Gerard Manley Hopkins. This variation is the curtal (*cf.* curtailed) sonnet, which retains the proportions of the two Petrarchan parts but reduces their size. A curtal sonnet, at least as written by Hopkins, consists of a six-line "octave" and a four-and-a-half-line "sestet," constructed according to the rhyme scheme *abcabc, dbcdc.* Hopkins wrote only two of these curtal sonnets, "Pied Beauty" and "Peace," and in many ways they are very fine poems; but for all their success, neither quite justifies itself as a structure—neither performs the fundamental Petrarchan action implicit in the formal disproportion of their two parts, an action of complication and resolution, or of something like it. Indeed, the two parts of "Pied Beauty," despite their presumably meaningful difference in weight and shape, are pretty much of a piece in substance, and we are left wondering what exactly in the action of the poem is justifying the form:

> Glory be to God for dappled things—
>   For skies of couple-colour as a brindled cow;
>   For rose-moles all in stipple upon trout that swim;
> Fresh-firecoal chestnut-falls; finches' wings;
>   Landscape plotted and pieced—fold, fallow, and plough;
>   And áll trádes, their gear and tackle and trim.

>All things counter, original, spare, strange;
>　Whatever is fickle, freckled (who knows how?)
>　　With swift, slow; sweet, sour; adazzle, dim;
>　He fathers-forth whose beauty is past change:
>　　　Praise him.

This is surely an exquisite poem, but it is not an exquisite "sonnet": the only thing that takes place in the white space between the two parts is an ascent to a slightly higher plateau of abstraction. The white space does not partake of the dramatic, as it does in a triumphant sonnet based on the plan of Petrarchan disproportion. What this means is that the poem fails to exploit its "sonnetness," which is another way of saying that it neglects one of its most open possibilities for attaining density. Hopkins seems to have forgotten to apply to the curtal sonnet his acute perception about the "downright prolapsus or hernia" that results from tying sestet to octave by rhyme.

The sonnet, of course, is only one of the English fixed forms, although it is probably among the best known. The fact that, like the limerick, it has meaning as a form alone is demonstrated by such a historical phenomenon as its lack of popularity among poets in the eighteenth century. These poets were acute enough to sense not merely that the sonnet as a form tends to imply a particular, highly personal, usually somewhat puzzled or worshipful attitude toward experience, but also—and more importantly—that they did not possess that attitude nor could affect it convincingly. It was for these reasons rather than because of any technical incompetence that they eschewed the sonnet and chose to work in other forms more expressive of their view of things and of themselves. Poetic forms are like that: they tend to say things even if words are not at the moment fitted to their patterns. As Louis MacNeice has said, "In any poet's poem the shape is half the meaning."

8

The English Stanzas

In thinking about English poetry, we must be careful to distinguish stanzaic forms from thematic kinds. For example, a thematic kind like the aubade, a traditional morning song expressing the disinclination of lovers to separate, may embody itself in any kind of stanzaic structure. The same is true of thematic kinds like the epigram, the elegy, the pastoral, the ode, and the song. It is true that certain stanzaic conventions tend to accompany certain kinds, but there is nothing in the nature of these kinds that makes a given stanza obligatory. Most satires are written in heroic couplets, but nothing in the satiric action prevents a satire's being composed in blank verse, or ballad stanzas, or any other stanzaic form.

When a poet is faced with decisions about organizing his materials, he has two large possibilities before him. He may choose a fixed form, or he may devise what we can call a nonce form. A fixed form is one that has been used many times before and whose conventions the reader is presumed to know. A nonce form is one invented for a single poetic occasion. Clearly all fixed forms have begun as nonce forms and have managed to prevail into history because in their shapes and in the conventions of their dynamics they have implied a version of experience recognized as real or significant or comely by many succeeding generations. The sonnet is a good example of this sort of fixed form; Hopkins's curtal sonnet is a nonce form which, we can say, has

never quite made the grade. When we want to speculate why
certain stanzaic forms have become fixed while others, which may
resemble them very closely, have not, we should probably inquire
less into any abstract aesthetic or mathematical theory than into
the psychological *données* of human nature. Certain stanzaic
forms have attained the eminence of fixity, less perhaps because
poets have liked to work in them than because readers have found
themselves gratified by them. No amount of brilliance on the part
of the performer will serve to make permanent a poetic form
which strikes the reader somehow as an unsatisfactory or insufficiently universal emblem of the shape of general psychic
experience.

The shape which a poetic stanza cuts in time was once, before
the widespread use of printing, apprehended by the ear alone.
In later times, the reader's conception of stanzaic form has been
both aural and visual. And now that we are fully accustomed
to using printed texts for apprehending poems, our sense of
stanzas has become a very complex act of mediation between what
our eyes see and what our inner ears hear. When we approach
a short poem on the printed page, the first thing that strikes us
is the general typographic shape that we are about to encounter:
we perceive first of all either a stichic accumulation or a stanzaic
organization, and the way we begin reading the poem will depend
in part on our first awareness of these typographic shapes and
on our sense of their general conventions. As we read along,
the aural experience gradually strengthens to confirm—if the
poem is good—the visual. And if the poem should happen to be
very good indeed, the visual and aural experiences of the poetic
form—the eye's measure of the physical shape and symbolism
of lines and stanzas, the ear's confirmation of the form given
to sounds by rhyme—will perfectly merge. When this happens,
we can say again that we are brought close to something like
the famous reconciliation of contraries which constitutes the
heart of Coleridge's aesthetic. It is interesting, incidentally, that
the great age of metrical variations in English poetry almost
exactly coincides with the age of printing, as if the joint work
of eye and inner ear necessitated by the reader's new encounter
with the printed page were all that was needed to reveal to
both poets and readers the new world of metrical delight based
on an aesthetic of pattern-and-variation. If we are skillful readers,

we will gradually learn to use our perceptions of stanzaic form to harmonize our senses of sight and of hearing, and thus perhaps to advance toward a heightened personal coherence analogous to the coherence of all the elements of a fully successful poem.

The basic stanzaic building blocks in English poetry are the couplet, the tercet, and the quatrain. Thus the Petrarchan sonnet can be seen as an arrangement of two quatrains and either two tercets or three couplets; the Shakespearean as an arrangement of three quatrains and a couplet. Since most of the complex English stanzas develop themselves simply by using variations or multiples of these three kinds of organization, it is well to begin with these simplest stanzaic elements.

The most rudimentary sort of stanzaic organization is the **couplet,** two lines of any length rhyming *aa.* Couplets whose lines are of the same length in feet are called equal couplets:

> How sleep the brave, who sink to rest,
> By all their country's wishes blest.

Those consisting of two lines of different foot-lengths are called unequal couplets:

> Hence with denial vain, and coy excuse,
> So may some gentle Muse
> With lucky words favour my destin'd Urn,
> And as he passes turn. . . .

Couplets in which the second line is stopped or retarded by strong punctuation at the end, and in which the first line exhibits a high degree of syntactical integrity, are called closed couplets:

> Faith is not built on disquisitions vain;
> The things we must believe are few and plain.

When enjambed, on the other hand, couplets are called open:

> That's my last Duchess painted on the wall,
> Looking as if she were alive. I call
> That piece a wonder, now: Frà Pandolf's hands
> Worked busily a day, and there she stands.

The most common lengths of couplets are tetrameter and pentameter. Tetrameter couplets are sometimes known as "short" couplets, and more frequently as octosyllabic couplets, although if bold substitutions occur few lines will accord with the octosyllabic ideal. Tetrameter couplets which rely on comical double (or "feminine") rhymes and on a pseudo-crude placement of stresses are often called Hudibrastic couplets in reference to their use by Samuel Butler in *Hudibras* (1662–1678) :

> When gospel-trumpeter, surrounded
> With long-eared rout, to battle sounded;
> And pulpit, drum ecclesiastic,
> Was beat with fist, instead of a stick. . . .

Pentameter couplets are called "heroic" because of their early association with heroic or epic subjects during the Restoration and the early eighteenth century: largely because of Dryden's and Pope's use of closed pentameter couplets in their famous translations of Virgil and Homer, the associations of the closed couplet have become more "heroic"—that is, elevated, operatic, "unrealistic"—than those of the open. To use a form associated with the elevated and the noble for rendering the plight of the low and pathetic, as Crabbe does in his closed-couplet narratives, is to exploit the associations of a verse form for ironic effect.

The difference between closed octosyllabic and closed heroic couplets might seem to be merely a difference in length. But the difference in length determines other important differences. For example, the octosyllabic couplet tends to circumscribe predication to its skeletal form of subject, verb, and object; it enforces a sparseness of modifiers:

> Had we but world enough and time,
> This coyness, lady, were no crime.

What happens when the octosyllabic couplet is expanded to the heroic is that adjectives and adverbs come flocking in. Thus the two sorts of couplets deal in very different textures: the texture of the octosyllabic couplet, regardless of who is writing in it, is likely to be lean and clean, spare and logical, a texture supremely appropriate to sarcasm or solid virile reasoning; the texture of the heroic couplet, with its abundant modifiers and qualifications, is likely to be more shaded, subtle, and busy.

Regardless of its length, the closed couplet seems both by its nature and its historical associations to imply something special about the materials enclosed in it. It seems to imply a distinct isolation of those materials from related things, a vigorous enclosure of them into a compact and momentarily self-sufficient little world of circumscribed sense and meaning. To construct a closed couplet is to draw a boundary line, to set something off as special and perhaps a trifle fragile. The couplet which concludes the Shakespearean sonnet often suggests this action, as do the epigrammatic couplets set into the middle of the "Essay on Man." One of the weaknesses of the Spenserian sonnet which we examined above is that it uses its internal couplets (especially its second one) in such a way that the logic tends to efface what the rhyme scheme tends to assert.

Three lines of any length ending with the same rhyme word are called **triplets,** or, interchangeably, **tercets.** It is probably better to use tercet only to distinguish three lines organized other than by a thrice-repeated rhyme. Thus this is a triplet:

> Whenas in silks my Julia goes,
> Then, then methinks how sweetly flows
> That liquefaction of her clothes,

but this is a tercet:

> O wild West Wind, thou breath of Autumn's being,
> Thou from whose unseen presence the leaves dead
> Are driven like ghosts from an enchanter fleeing. . . .

The triplet is not nearly so popular among English poets as the couplet, and the reason is not far to seek. The same rhyme sound repeated in sequence without relief tends to produce fatiguing and sometimes comic or bizarre effects: the triplet has enough rhymes just to risk this danger. Indeed, its number of sequential rhymes is probably as great as we can stand without inviting monotony or comedy. If we add a line to Herrick's triplet, we can see what may happen:

> Whenas in silks my Julia goes,
> In shiny handkercher and hose,
> Then, then methinks how sweetly flows
> That liquefaction of her clothes.

It is a little too much, like sucking a series of sugar cubes.

Iambic pentameter triplets are sometimes used in heroic couplet poems to mark moments of climax or special pressure, and often the last line of the triplet swells to an alexandrine, as if the materials were stretching their container and almost bursting out of confinement. Thus the end of Swift's "A Description of a City Shower," where the "torrents" of refuse

> . . . in huge confluence joined at Snow Hill ridge,
> Fall from the conduit prone to Holborn Bridge.
> Sweepings from butchers' stalls, dung, guts, and blood,
> Drowned puppies, stinking sprats, all drenched in mud,
> Dead cats and turnip tops come tumbling down the flood.

One tercet stanza which has never really established itself in English is the *terza rima,* the stanza of Dante's *Divine Comedy.* The tercets rhyme *aba, bcb, cdc,* and so on, each tercet beginning and ending with the center rhyme of the tercet preceding. In Dante the line length is five iambic feet with an extra syllable, but English poets have utilized the *terza rima* in various line lengths, from the tetrameters of Browning's "The Statue and the Bust" to the loose pentameters of Shelley's "Ode to the West Wind." The failure of *terza rima* to establish a tradition in English, as well as the general rarity of successful English three-line stanzas, suggests that stanzas of even- rather than odd-numbered lines are those that appeal most naturally to the Anglo-Saxon sensibility. We may inquire how well any three-line stanza, regardless of the talent of its practitioner, can ever succeed in English.

An even more exotic version of the tercet is the *haiku* (or *hokku*), a tiny and reputedly exquisite form imported from Japan. The most common *haiku* is a syllabic tercet whose three lines contain five, seven (or eight), and five syllables. Playing around with it in English is surely as harmless as working crossword puzzles; but since its structural principles seem to have very little to do with the nature of the English language, we should not expect the form to produce any memorable poems. Here is a *haiku* translated by Harold G. Henderson from the original by Taniguchi Buson:

> The short night is through:
> on the hairy caterpillar,
> little beads of dew.

If triplets and tercets tend to remain awkward rarities among English stanzas, **quatrains**—stanzas of four lines—are the most popular and "natural" strophic form. Most of the actual poems that ordinary people remember (and recite) are written in quatrains, as are most common mnemonic verses, nursery rhymes, rhymed saws and proverbs and admonitions, hymns, and popular songs. The unsophisticated person's experience of poetry is almost equivalent to his experience of quatrains, which tends to suggest that there is something in four-line stanzaic organization (or in the principle of alternate rhyming) that projects a deep and permanent appeal to those whose language is English. The presence of the quatrain at the heart of the sonnet bespeaks its appeal to the sophisticated as well. If we destroyed all English poetry written in quatrains—as well as that written in blank verse and heroic couplets—what would remain would resemble the literary corpus of, say, Luxembourg.

The simplest quatrain is the ballad stanza, consisting usually of alternating iambic tetrameter and trimeter lines rhyming *abcb:*

> Western wind, when will thou blow
> The small rain down can rain?
> Christ, if my love were in my arms
> And I in my bed again!

A tighter variant uses two sets of rhymes:

> If all the world were sought so far,
> Who could find such a wight?
> Her beauty twinkleth like a star
> Within a frosty night.

When ballad stanza is used for hymns it is called common (or short) measure:

> Oh! for a closer walk with God
> A calm and heavenly frame;
> A light to shine upon the road
> That leads me to the Lamb!

If lines 2 and 4 are also tetrameters like lines 1 and 3, the stanza, now a tetrameter quatrain, is called long measure:

> When I survey the wondrous cross
> On which the Prince of Glory died,
> My richest gain I count but loss,
> And pour contempt on all my pride.

One of the conventions associated with the ballad or hymnal stanzas is an illusion of primitive sincerity and openness. By using such a stanza for highly sophisticated and knowing or sardonic purposes, as Emily Dickinson frequently did and as Eliot does in "Sweeney Among the Nightingales," a poet can cause the bare stanza itself to contribute mightily to his irony.

Another variant of the tetrameter quatrain is what we can call the couplet quatrain:

> That which her slender waist confined
> Shall now my joyful temples bind;
> No monarch but would give his crown
> His arms might do what this has done.

And when we add a foot to the lines of a tetrameter quatrain with alternate rhymes, we seem to add weight and solemnity, and we end with the so-called heroic or elegiac quatrain. It is sometimes called heroic because of its association with noble subjects during the Restoration. Dryden's "Annus Mirabilis" provides good examples of one sort of materials that most readers will associate with the heroic quatrain:

> To nearest Ports their shatter'd Ships repair,
> Where by our dreadful Canon they lay aw'd:
> So reverently Men quit the open air,
> When Thunder speaks the angry Gods abroad.

The term heroic quatrain is also applied to a four-line stanza formed from two heroic couplets.

The *abab* iambic pentameter quatrain is also called elegiac, probably because of Gray's "Elegy Written in a Country Church-yard," which imparts great dignity to the stanza:

> Nor you, ye Proud, impute to These the fault,
> If Mem'ry o'er their Tomb no Trophies raise,
> Where thro' the long-drawn isle and fretted vault
> The pealing anthem swells the note of praise.

So powerfully are elegiac instincts associated by now with the iambic pentameter quatrain, the stanza not merely of Gray's "Elegy" but of Fitzgerald's sardonic *Rubaiyat* as well, that a highly literary poet like Allen Tate can superadd a dimension of meaning by using it for modern ironic elegies like his "Mr. Pope" or "Death of Little Boys," just as John Crowe Ransom does in "Dead Boy," or as Richard Eberhart does in the last stanza of "The Fury of Aerial Bombardment."

Another well-known kind of quatrain is the so-called In Memoriam stanza, named after its popularization by Tennyson's *In Memoriam* (1850). Here the rhyming principle is that of the quatrains in the Petrarchan sonnet, the principle of enclosure. The four tetrameter lines rhyme *abba,* and we have an effect of an external couplet gripping an internal one:

> To-night ungathered let us leave
>   This laurel, let this holly stand:
>   We live within the stranger's land,
> And strangely falls our Christmas-eve.

One interesting characteristic of the In Memoriam stanza is the illusion of powerful emphasis which the end of line 3 seems to receive because of the contiguity of its rhyme word with the rhyme word of line 2. Sometimes Tennyson's adaptation of his sense to this structural peculiarity of the stanza is very telling, as in this famous example, where he contrives that the semantic and structural climaxes shall coincide exactly:

> That God, which ever lives and loves,
>   One God, one law, one element,
>   And one far-off divine event,
> To which the whole creation moves.

That this accumulation of force at the end of line 3 is a characteristic attaching more to the stanza than to Tennyson is apparent in these stanzas from Ben Jonson's "An Elegie":

> And you are he: the Deitie
>   To whom all lovers are design'd;
>   That would their better objects find:
> Among which faithfull troope am I.
>
> Who as an off-spring at your shrine,
>   Have sung this Hymne, and here intreat
>   One sparke of your Diviner heat
> To light upon a Love of mine.
>
> Which if it kindle not, but scant
>   Appeare, and that to shortest view,
>   You give me leave t'adore in you
> What I, in her, am griev'd to want.

Other nineteenth-century poets such as Clough and Rossetti also used the In Memoriam stanza, but it is now so closely associated with the sturdy, serviceable elegiac atmosphere of *In Memoriam* itself that it has shared the fate of the Spenserian stanza: it evokes the poem with which it is associated so powerfully that its uses now seem limited to occasions which either resemble or mock the original.

Another fairly popular fixed form of the quatrain is the Sapphic stanza, which is an attempt to reproduce in English the original stanza of Sappho, a stanza used also by Catullus and Horace. The English Sapphic stanza seems more successful than other imitations of classical forms. It consists of three eleven-syllable lines—hendecasyllables—followed by a five-syllable line; the stresses of the hendecasyllables imitate by dactyls and trochees the quantities of the classical original, with a spondee (or trochee) falling customarily in the second position. Thus Isaac Watts in "The Day of Judgment":

> When the fierce north wind with his airy forces
> Rears up the Baltic to a foaming fury,
> And the red lightning with a storm of hail comes
>   Rushing amain down,

How the poor sailors stand amazed and tremble,
While the hoarse thunder, like a bloody trumpet,
Roars a loud onset to the gaping waters,
 Quick to devour them!

The final short line, an invariable sign of the Sapphic or the Sapphic-derived quatrain, is composed always, in a "pure" Sapphic, of a dactyl and a trochee. One disadvantage of the Sapphic stanza is just this relative inflexibility of meter: part of the achievement in a Sapphic consists in imitating the arbitrary classical quantities as exactly as possible, and yet, as we have seen, to follow a predetermined stress pattern is to reject that whole vast dimension of meaning and suggestion which is the province of metrical variations.

This disadvantage of the Sapphic stanza is avoided by more boldly Anglicized versions like George Herbert's "Virtue," a poem which retains the proportions of the classical Sapphic but domesticates the stanza by reducing the three long lines to tetrameters and by establishing an iambic base against which meaningful substitution can occur:

> Sweet day, so cool, so calm, so bright!
> The bridal of the earth and sky—
> The dew shall weep thy fall to-night;
> For thou must die.
>
> Sweet rose, whose hue angry and brave
> Bids the rash gazer wipe his eye,
> Thy root is ever in its grave,
> And thou must die. . . .

Another happy performance in a version of the Sapphic stanza is Pope's "Ode on Solitude," where we have an exquisite adaptation of the sense to the lesser weight of the final half-line:

> Happy the man, whose wish and care
> A few paternal acres bound,
> Content to breathe his native air
> In his own ground.

> Whose herds with milk, whose fields with bread,
> Whose flocks supply him with attire,
> Whose trees in summer yield him shade,
>   In winter fire. . . .

On the other hand, the variant employed by Coleridge in "Love,"
with its final line lengthened to three feet, seems less successful:
there seems to be a kind of crudity and overinsistence in the excessively weighted final line, although the crudity may really be
the effect of simply an insufficiently varied metric:

> All thoughts, all passions, all delights,
> Whatever stirs this mortal frame,
> All are but ministers of Love,
>   And feed his sacred flame.
>
> Oft in my waking dreams do I
> Live o'er again that happy hour,
> When midway on the mount I lay,
>   Beside the ruin'd tower. . . .

Because of its inevitable associations with the poems of Sappho,
the Sapphic stanza, and even fairly distant pseudo-Sapphic variations of it, seems to imply a certain passion and seriousness:
frivolity and comedy and wit are not among its conventions.

Immense frivolity, on the other hand, is the inseparable ac-
cessory of the four-line stanza called the clerihew, a whimsical
kind of quatrain devised by Edmund Clerihew Bentley early in
the present century. A clerihew consists of two couplets—usually
with whimsical rhymes—of any line length, the more unequal
the better. Most clerihews are about people, and the convention
is that the subject's name constitutes the first line. Here is one of
Bentley's clerihews:

> John Stuart Mill
> By a mighty effort of will
> Overcame his natural bonhomie
> And wrote *Principles of Political Economy*.

And here is one celebrating one of the greatest of British
cricketers, whose trademark was his full beard:

> W. G. Grace
> Had hair all over his face.
> Lord, how the people cheered
> When the ball got lost in his beard.

(The initial trochaic substitution in line 3 is not the least attractive element of this tiny masterpiece.)

These are the main varieties of the quatrain, the workhorse stanza of English poetry. So closely, indeed, is the very idea of the quatrain associated with the notion of poetry that four lines of anything—even dashes or numbers—grouped on a page will instantly look like a "poem," while three or five similar lines will risk resembling an abstract design or a secret code. The archetype of the quatrain has been retained even by poets who have totally abandoned its rationale of rhyme. Thus Ted Hughes in "View of a Pig":

> Once I ran at a fair in the noise
> To catch a greased piglet
> That was faster and nimbler than a cat,
> Its squeal was the rending of metal.

Faced with an example like this, we can suggest that if a fusion of both visual shape and auditory structure is what makes a stanza, a poet like Hughes has overbalanced the merely visual and has thus overemphasized inharmoniously one element of the dualistic stanzaic experience at the expense of the other. What he produces is very nice, but his stanza surely lacks the dense organicism that attaches to a permanent poem.

With the exception of the limerick—and the so-called "mad song," which we shall consider shortly—English offers no conventional fixed form of a **five-line stanza**. Many nonce arrangements are possible. The most attractive kinds of five-line organization seem to involve the envelope principle, the principle of enclosure or return, as in the limerick (*aabba*), where the closure of the final sense is coincident with the sound closure echoing the initial rhymes. The structure is analogous to a musical structure which begins in a major key, shifts to minor, and finally returns—gratifyingly, we have been brought up to feel—to major. Other possibilities of enclosure patterns in five lines are *abbba,* *aaaba,* and *ababa.* Sir Philip Sidney's "Eleventh Song" is a pleasant example of this last:

> Who is it that this dark night
> Underneath my window plaineth?
>   It is one who from thy sight
>   Being, ah, exiled, disdaineth
> Every other vulgar light.

Here the logical relation of the rhymes is almost as close as their sound relation, with the *light* of the second voice beautifully closing the *night* of the first. We can contrast the very different kind of effect resulting from a five-line pattern which does not exploit the enclosure principle. This *abccb* stanza is from Wordsworth's "Peter Bell":

> Beneath the clear blue sky he saw
> A little field of meadow ground;
> But field or meadow name it not;
> Call it of earth a small green plot,
> With rocks encompassed round.

This is essentially the In Memoriam stanza with an additional line at the beginning. The four lines which constitute the enclosure action of the structure grip together nicely, but the first line, for whose echoing rhyme unconsciously we look in vain, tends to drift away, to separate itself from that to which the typography tells us it is structurally indispensable. We end with feelings of a vague structural uneasiness: we are not satisfied and fulfilled as we seem to be by the structure of Sidney's five-line arrangement.

The structure of Wordsworth's "Peter Bell" stanza is actually a variant of the conventional "mad-song" stanza, a stanza associated since the early Renaissance with a traditional poem sung by a madman. Here is an example from an anonymous sixteenth-century "Tom o' Bedlam's Song":

> I know more than Apollo,
>   For, oft when he lies sleeping,
>   I behold the stars
>   At bloody wars,
> And the wounded welkin weeping.

And here it is again, still lively over a century later in the hands of Thomas D'Urfey:

> I'll sail upon the dog-star,
>   And then pursue the morning;
>   I'll chase the moon
>   Till it be noon,
> But I'll make her leave her horning.

This stanza had for three centuries a distinct expressive advantage: like most fixed forms, it meant something in and by itself. It connoted immediately a happy, harmless, and verbally inventive brand of insanity, just as the rhythm and structure of the limerick stanza in our time connote ideas of wild geography, anticlericalism, and bizarre indecency.

Another five-line possibility is to join a triplet to a couplet, as Rossetti does in "Rose Mary":

> Mary mine that art Mary's Rose,
> Come in to me from the garden-close.
> The sun sinks fast with rising dew,
> And we marked not how the faint moon grew;
> But the hidden stars are calling you.

All we can say about this is that if a poet wants his five-line stanza to fracture into two parts each time, this is the structure to use. Similar disadvantages seem to attach to other five-line patterns in which the enclosure principle does not operate, although the stanzas of Wyatt's "The Lover Complaineth the Unkindness of His Love," with the pattern *aabab*, cohere nicely, partly because the *a*'s are interlocked with the *b*'s:

> Now cease, my lute, this is the last
> Labor that thou and I shall waste,
> And ended is that we begun.
> Now is this song both sung and past,
> My lute, be still, for I have done.

The most common **six-line stanzas** are those either of three couplets or of a quatrain and a couplet. An example of the first is William Oldys's "On a Fly Drinking from His Cup":

> Busy, curious, thirsty fly!
> Drink with me, and drink as I:
> Freely welcome to my cup,
> Couldst thou sip and sip it up:
> Make the most of life you may,
> Life is short and wears away.

We find the second in Wordsworth's "I Wandered Lonely as a Cloud":

> I wandered lonely as a cloud
> That floats on high o'er vales and hills,
> When all at once I saw a crowd,
> A Host, of golden daffodils;
> Beside the lake, beneath the trees,
> Fluttering and dancing in the breeze.

When the lines of Wordsworth's stanza are lengthened by a foot to pentameter, we have the so-called Venus and Adonis stanza, named after Shakespeare's poem:

> Over one arm the lusty courser's rein,
> Under her other was the tender boy,
> Who blush'd and pouted in a dull disdain,
> With leaden appetite, unapt to toy;
>   She red and hot as coals of glowing fire,
>   He red for shame, but frosty in desire.

We can observe here the way the final heroic couplet, as it does in the Shakespearean sonnet, tempts the poet who arrives at it after the quatrain to sallies of epigrammatic paradox, witty commentary, and tongue-in-cheek hyperbole which seem to inhabit a different world from that with which the quatrain concerns itself. This is one way poetic structure in the hands of a master often supports and in part even triggers what is being said.

Another common six-line stanza is the tail rhyme or *rime couée,* associated with many Middle English romances and with Chaucer's parody of them in "The Tale of Sir Thopas." The standard form is two tetrameter couplets followed by semantically attached trimeters, the whole rhyming *aabccb,* as in Wordsworth's "To a Young Lady, Who Had Been Reproached for Taking Long Walks in the Country":

Dear Child of Nature, let them rail!
—There is a nest in a green dale,
　　A harbour and a hold;
Where thou, a Wife and Friend, shalt see
Thy own heart-stirring days, and be
　　A light to young and old.

Although it is most often found in the six-line form, the tail-rhyme principle appears in stanzas of various lengths, and almost infinite variations are possible. One, for example, is the nine-line stanza of Tennyson's "The Lady of Shalott" ($aaaa^4b^3ccc^4b^3$). Another is the highly flexible stanza of Tennyson's "Charge of the Light Brigade."

The most conspicuous master of the tail-rhyme stanza in English is probably Robert Burns, who uses that variant of it called Standard Habbie, named after a Renaissance poem lamenting the death of Habbie Simson, the renowned piper of Kilbarchan. Standard Habbie is a six-line stanza containing two dimeter "bobs" or "tails," one following a triplet of iambic tetrameters and one following a final iambic tetrameter. The rhyme scheme is *aaabab*. Sometimes the bob-lines are used to add a final overlay of tenderness, as in "To a Mountain Daisy":

Wee modest crimson-tipped flow'r,
Thou'st met me in an evil hour;
For I maun crush amang the stoure
　　Thy slender stem:
To spare thee now is past my pow'r,
　　Thou bonnie gem.

But more often the bobs are used as fillips of impudent irony. In "Holy Willie's Prayer," for example, Mr. William Fisher, one of the worthies of the local kirk given to disciplining Burns for his sexual indiscipline, is made to confess his own backslidings:

O Lord! yestreen, thou kens, wi' Meg—
Thy pardon I sincerely beg;
O! May't ne'er be a livin' plague
　　To my dishonour,
An' I'll ne'er lift a lawless leg
　　Again upon her.

These effects would hardly be possible except in short lines, which beautifully serve to drop the high-flown abruptly into reality. The bob performs a similar deflating function in "The Holy Fair," where it terminates an eight-line arrangement consisting of two ballad stanzas:

> How mony hearts this day converts
>   O' sinners and o' lasses!
> Their hearts o' stane, gin night, are gane
>   As saft as ony flesh is.
> There's some are fou o' love divine;
>   There's some are fou o' brandy;
> An' mony jobs that day begin,
>   May end in houghmagandie
>   Some ither day.

But Burns's ways of managing the bob are almost as various as his poems themselves. Sometimes he shows off by letting the bob carry on the syntax of the longer lines with scarcely a break so that it ceases to stand as a witty attachment or pseudo-after-thought and functions instead as simply a wittily structured continuation of the original stanzaic fabric. This is the way he uses it, and with great skill, in his "Epistle to John Lapraik, An Old Scottish Bard":

> What's a' your jargon o' your schools,
> Your Latin names for horns and stools:
> If honest nature made you fools,
>   What sairs your grammars?
> Ye'd better ta'en up spades and shools,
>   Or knappin'-hammers.
>
> A set o' dull, conceited hashes
> Confuse their brains in college classes!
> They gang in stirks, and come out asses,
>   Plain truth to speak;
> And syne they think to climb Parnassus
>   By dint o' Greek!
>
> Gie me ae spark o' Nature's fire,
> That's a' the learning I desire;

> Then tho' I drudge thro' dub an' mire
> At pleugh or cart,
> My Muse, though hamely in attire,
> May touch the heart.

A final kind of six-line stanza is that which appears in the sestina, a complicated Italian and French form of perhaps dubious structural expressiveness in English. The sestina consists of six six-line stanzas and a final three-line stanza: the stanzas are constructed not by terminal rhyme but by the repetition in an elaborate established order of the six terminal words. The standard arrangement of the terminal words looks like this: *abcdef, faebdc, cfdabe, ecbfad, deacfb, bdfeca, eca.* The sestina has attracted some nineteenth- and twentieth-century poets, including Swinburne, Kipling, Auden, and Pound; and R. P. Blackmur, in "Mr. Virtue and the Three Bears," has produced what he calls "a masquerade of a sestina" by repeating in the successive stanzas the terminal words in the same order in which they stand in the first. But like many imported forms, the sestina, regardless of the way it is tailored, would seem to be one that gives more structural pleasure to the contriver than to the apprehender.

The most important fixed form of the **seven-line stanzas** is *rime royale,* an iambic-pentameter stanza rhyming *ababbcc:* it consists of a heroic quatrain and one and one-half heroic couplets. It is associated with the narration of high and noble matters. Chaucer used it in "Troilus and Criseyde," "The Parlement of Foules," "The Clerk's Tale," and "The Man of Law's Tale"; Shakespeare used it to tell the story of "The Rape of Lucrece"; and it was used also by Wyatt and King James I. Like the imaginative world of romance and the erotic-heroic with which it is associated, the stanza flourished from the end of the Middle Ages to the end of the sixteenth century, and since then has been revived only occasionally, and by such as William Morris and John Masefield.

The *rime royale* stanza is capable of great unity, partly because of the way the central couplet overlaps the initial quatrain, and partly because the effect of the final separated couplet is prepared for gradually by the central couplet. The stanza's progression from quatrain to couplet organization is thus subtle and gradual, fully prepared for by structural means. Shakespeare's "Rape of Lucrece" provides good examples:

> Without the bed her other fair hand was,
> On the green coverlet; whose perfect white
> Show'd like an April daisy on the grass,
> With pearly sweat resembling dew of night.
> Her eyes, like marigolds, had sheath'd their light,
> And canopied in darkness sweetly lay,
> Till they might open to adorn the day.

One way of forming **eight-line stanzas** is by fusing two quatrains and rhyming either *ababcdcd* or *abababab*. Variations involving a combination of a quatrain and two couplets are also common, as are simple accumulations of four couplets. But the most popular fixed form of eight-line stanza is *ottava rima,* consisting of an iambic pentameter stanza rhyming *abababcc.* Imported from Italy by Wyatt, this stanza was in high vogue during the Renaissance, when it was used by Sidney, Spenser, Daniel, Harington, Drayton, and Fairfax. Byron's *Don Juan* is now the poem which most readers would associate with *ottava rima,* and in that poem we can appreciate one of the rare miracles by which a poet's individual genius and a single stanzaic form encounter each other in delight and end in an eminently fruitful marriage. It is both the virtue and the defect of Byron's talent that he has a profound instinct for making comments, for deflating units of narrative with moments of satiric observation. The *ottava rima,* like both the Venus and Adonis stanza and the Shakespearean sonnet, which it resembles in structure, is the perfect form for the indulgence of a talent like Byron's. The stanza itself, with its six lines of interlocked, unified preparation followed by its couplet of climax, release, or commentary, constitutes a paradigm of inflation and deflation, or of the heroic which swells and swells until it bursts into the mock-heroic. The stanza is an appropriate vehicle for a poem which, as Byron said, is "meant to be a little quietly facetious upon everything." The very rhyme scheme implies that each stanza will contain two more or less distinct kinds of materials, and few stanzas disappoint our structural expectations:

Sagest of women, even of widows, she
  Resolved that Juan should be quite a paragon,
And worthy of the noblest pedigree:
  (His sire was of Castile, his dam from Aragon).
Then for accomplishments of chivalry,
  In case our lord the king should go to war again,
He learn'd the arts of riding, fencing, gunnery,
And how to scale a fortress—or a nunnery.

  . . .

I had my doubts, perhaps I have them still,
  But what I say is neither here nor there:
I knew his father well, and have some skill
  In character—but it would not be fair
From sire to son to augur good or ill:
  He and his wife were an ill-sorted pair—
But scandal's my aversion—I protest
Against all evil speaking, even in jest.

The chief of the **nine-line stanzas** is the Spenserian, the vehicle of *The Faerie Queene*. The stanza consists of eight iambic-pentameter lines rhyming *ababbcbc* and a final alexandrine rhyming *c*. Spenser perhaps contrived the stanza by adding the final rhyming alexandrine to the eight lines of the stanza of Chaucer's "Monk's Tale," which also rhymes *ababbcbc*. Wherever he derived his stanza, the addition of the final alexandrine is Spenser's bold stroke: the very inequality of the final couplet helps alleviate much of the tediousness that a fixed stanza risks when used for prolonged narrative. And the quatrain and couplet patterns are closely merged by the repeated rhymes, one in the middle of the stanza, one at the end: we get the illusion that the couplets are being brought forth from the quatrains rather than superadded to them. The two fundamentally different kinds of structure take on an almost magical vesture of homogeneity:

Eftsoones they heard a most melodious sound,
  Of all that mote delight a daintie eare,
  Such as attonce might not on liuing ground,
  Saue in this Paradise, be heard elswhere:
  Right hard it was, for wight, which did it heare,
  To read, what manner musicke that mote bee:
  For all that pleasing is to liuing eare,
  Was there consorted in one harmonee,
Birdes, voyces, instruments, windes, waters, all agree.

The Spenserian stanza is not used alone for lyric purposes: it is found primarily as a narrative vehicle, making its effects by small variations on the often repeated basic pattern. During the eighteenth century a vogue of Spenserian imitation resulted in several pseudo-Spenserian poems such as Shenstone's "The Schoolmistress" and Thomson's "The Castle of Indolence," and Burns used the stanza in his unfortunate Anglicized "Cotter's Saturday Night."

But it was Keats, in "The Eve of St. Agnes," who brought the requisite prosodic taste to the Spenserian stanza and succeeded so well in it that, in effect, no one has dared to write in it since. Tennyson did venture to open "The Lotos-Eaters" with five Spenserian stanzas, and a few other nineteenth-century poets exercised themselves in the form, but none could equal Keats's triumphs, or even come close. And even Keats did not learn all at once how to make the stanza his own. His boyish, insecure "Imitation of Spenser," with its cautious end-stopped prosody, doggedly fills up with inert materials the receptacles offered by the stanza. Within seven years the stanza no longer dominates Keats: he commands it, and he commands it with a kind of security and originality that very few poets—even (dare one say it?) Spenser himself—have ever brought to a stanzaic form:

> Then by the bed-side, where the faded moon
>   Made a dim, silver twilight, soft he set
>   A table, and, half anguish'd, threw thereon
>   A cloth of woven crimson, gold, and jet:—
>   O for some drowsy Morphean amulet!
>   The boisterous, midnight, festive clarion,
>   The kettle-drum, and far-heard clarinet,
>   Affray his ears, though but in dying tone:—
> The hall door shuts again and all the noise is gone.
>
> And still she slept an azure-lidded sleep,
>   In blanchèd linen, smooth and lavender'd,
>   While he from forth the closet brought a heap
>   Of candied apple, quince, and plum, and gourd;
>   With jellies soother than the creamy curd,
>   And lucent syrops, tinct with cinnamon;
>   Manna and dates, in argosy transferr'd
>   From Fez; and spiced dainties, every one
> From silken Samarcand to cedar'd Lebanon.

It is undeniable that much of what is transmitted here is the result of exotic diction, almost alone. And yet it would be difficult to miss the part of the effect that develops and accelerates from the relation of the syntax to the stanzaic form. The enjambment, so bold and controlled at once, delicately opposes the rhyme sanctions of the stanza at the same time that it recognizes them and invites us to respect them. And the technical triumph of the whole passage is probably the treatment of the alexandrine which closes the first stanza and the all-important door of the lovers at once. From noise to absolute silence—from pentameter to hexameter, and then to white space: the form reinforces the sense with such delicacy and taste that we dissolve in delight— or so Keats, in his structural wisdom, assumes we will.

Between the nine lines of the Spenserian stanza and the fourteen of the sonnet, English offers no conventional fixed forms; although accumulations of three quatrains are popular, the conventions of such arrangements attach to the quatrain rather than to any twelve-line conception. And in English we have no fixed stanzaic form longer than the sonnet.

The availability of fixed forms, and a poet's relation to them, are always very complex matters. The poet always faces choices, but in some ages more choices will invite him than in others. And even though the forms can be said to persist always, in a world of pure idea, some forms are usable at certain times but not at others. It is taste and nothing else that will urge the poet toward certain fixed forms and away from others. Knowing what the very form implies in and of itself, regardless of what is done with it, is one of the poet's guides. We have already seen that the eighteenth-century poet tended to eschew the sonnet; he did this in the way that the nineteenth-century poet avoided the closed heroic couplet, or the twentieth-century poet avoids the Spenserian stanza.

One of the most obvious differences between modern poetry and that of only sixty or seventy years ago is the abandonment of most of the more complex English fixed forms and the loosening of the others. One widely read modern anthology, John Malcolm Brinnin and Bill Read's *The Modern Poets* (1963), prints 201 poems. Although this is an anthology which leans toward a conservative taste in matters of "clarity" and form, only about 37 per cent of the poems are written in fixed forms or in traditional stichic patterns. The most popular form is loose blank verse, often ordered into verse paragraphs of unequal size. In this way many of the poets pay their prosodic respects to Yeats. The next most popular form is the tetrameter quatrain, the stanza of Eliot's "Sweeney Among the Nightingales." Third in popularity is the elegiac quatrain, which is often used ironically or almost mock-heroically. In the whole collection we find only three sonnets, one Shakespearean and two modifications of the Petrarchan. Five poems are in Swiftian-Yeatsian tetrameter couplets; two are in loose heroic couplets; four are in ballad stanza; one is in *terza rima,* one is in the Venus and Adonis stanza, and one is in the In Memoriam stanza. But the great bulk of the poems are either in nonce stanzas or in continuous stichic form with occasional but not patterned rhyme.

And the Brinnin and Read collection is traditionally oriented. If we should turn instead to Donald M. Allen's *The New American Poetry: 1945–1960,* a collection of "Beat" and primitivist work revealing the multiple paternity of Whitman, William Carlos Williams, and the Pound of the later *Cantos,* we encounter an all but total rejection of traditional stanzaic and stichic forms, and an attitude toward rhyme as a formal device which can be described only as a programmatic hostility. Indeed, the Allen anthology contains 209 poems, and only six of them use patterned rhyme, although a very few more use occasional rhymes for emphasis or embellishment. Of the six poems in traditional stanzaic arrangements, four are in tetrameter couplets, one is in tetrameter couplets and triplets, and one is in a vaguely Sapphic stanza rhyming *abcb.* In place of the customary attention to the ends of lines in the rhyming tradition, we see a curious attempt to shift the prosodic emphasis back to the beginnings of lines: the favored device for executing this shift is initial syntactical repetition derived largely from Whitman: it is used instead of rhyme by Lawrence Ferlinghetti, Allen Ginsberg, Lew Welch, Philip Lamantia, and others.

A more recent anthology, presenting not Beats now but sophisticated professional "creative writing" university poets all under the age of forty, registers the continuing flight from traditional meter and forms. Daniel Halpern's *The American Poetry Anthology* (1975), said by its publisher to exhibit "the best poetry written in recent years," contains 313 poems by 76 poets. Fewer than 2½ percent depend on anything like fixed forms or a meter of grid and variation. Only seven poems use end-rhyme in any way, usually near-rhyme or simply a hint of assonance at line-endings. There are two things called "sonnets," each in 15 lines (for no visible reason) ; the lines are unrhymed, and thus offer no formal rationale distinguishing octave from sestet. There are a number of pseudo-quatrains without rhyme—the convention that a quatrain looks like poetry dies hard—and one lonely pseudo-Sapphic. Otherwise the poems, many of them delightful in theme and diction and perception and complexity of tone, are shapeless and thus unmemorable. If we conceive of the English traditional forms as analogous in some ways to the wing collar, the poems in Halpern's anthology are not quite like the tee-shirts of the Beats—they are more like nice button-downs, clean and perfectly presentable, but notably without starch.

A few of the "Beat" poets have essayed interesting critical justifications of their technical usages, although not all of their critical remarks go as far as Ginsberg commenting on the formal shape of *Howl:* "A lot of these forms developed out of an extreme rhapsodic wail I once heard in a madhouse." Perhaps a more useful observation is Robert Duncan's ascription of the "Beat" attitude toward traditional form to the contemporary assumption of the force of the unconscious: "After Freud," he says, "we are aware that unwittingly we achieve our form." Whether a reflection of psychological or social revolution, clearly something important has happened to the poet's posture toward received poetic forms.

What it is has been suggested by J. V. Cunningham in "The Problem of Form." The poet's attitude toward fixed metrical and stanzaic forms, Cunningham reminds us, reflects his general orientation toward authority, hierarchy, and history; and the contemporary poet, anxious to escape from the fixed forms, is conducting his own small skirmish in the continuing romantic and democratic revolutions. But a poetry without a memory of its fixed forms, Cunningham reasons, abandons a dimension of meaning that perhaps it cannot afford to lose. As he says:

Prose is written in sentences; poetry in sentences and lines. It is encoded not only in grammar, but also simultaneously in meter, for meter

is the principle or set of principles, whatever they may be, that determine the line. . . . We have lost the repetitive harmony of the old
tradition, and we have not established a new. We have written to vary
or violate the old line, for regularity we feel is meaningless and irregularity meaningful. But a generation of poets, acting on the principles and practice of significant variation, have at last nothing to vary
from. . . .

And yet, even though we know all this, the problem has no
apparent solution. The contemporary poet will not write in
stanzas like the sonnet, or the Venus and Adonis, or the In
Memoriam—fixed forms which are irretrievably associated with
the opposite of what he himself wants to register about experience. For him to use even a form so devoid of specific
thematic and emotional associations as, say, the tetrameter
quatrain is to imply an attitude toward order and reason and
the predictable and the recurrent which today he probably will
not want his poem to imply.

But the other horn of the dilemma is equally painful. Poetry
is form, and permanent poetry is permanent form. And by "form"
here we mean that pattern which works on the reader and is
recognized by him, no matter how unconsciously or irrationally,
to constitute a significant abstract repetitive frame; we do not
mean an idiosyncratic pattern—the mere number of syllables
per line, for example—which may justify itself mathematically
and theoretically, but which does not prove itself upon the pulses
of readers. Some kind of meaningful repetition would seem to
be required to save a poem from oblivion. The challenge to
contemporary poetry would seem to be a pair of unhappy alternatives; either to contrive new schemes of empirically meaningful
repetition that reflect and—more importantly—transmit the color
of contemporary experience; or to recover schemes that have reflected the experience of the past. To do the first would be to
imply that contemporary experience has a pattern, a point that
most post-Christian thinkers would deny. To do the second
would be to suggest that the past can be recaptured, to suggest
that the intolerable fractures and dislocations of modern history
have not really occurred at all, or, what is worse, to suggest that
they may have occurred but that poetry should act as if they
have not. Between these two demands of accuracy of registration,

on the one hand, and aesthetic organization, on the other, we seem to find no technique of reconciliation: we yield now to the one demand, now to the other, producing at times a formless and artistically incoherent reflection—accurate in its way—of some civil or social or psychological reality, and at times a shapely and coherent work of art which is necessarily an inexact report on the state of affairs, not to mention the state of language and meaning and coherence, in our time. If J. V. Cunningham seeks to recall contemporary poets to an awareness that without form there is no poem, Ginsberg retorts: "I hear ghostly Academics in Limbo screeching about form." If Ginsberg and D. H. Lawrence and Hart Crane sacrifice to the first demand, Frost and Auden and Wilbur sacrifice to the second. What is wanted is the sort of reconciliation between them that could be effected by another Yeats.

9

Some Critical Implications
of Stanzaic Forms

It should neither surprise nor distress us that most poetry in English ranges from the mediocre to the very bad and that most poets are technically incompetent. So are most waiters, physicians, carpenters, lawyers, gardeners, and teachers. The genuinely successful poems to which we return again and again constitute a tiny selection from the vast and almost measureless rubbish heap of the centuries. Anyone with access to a good library who has read assiduously in the now entirely unrecalled poetic effusions of the last three centuries—the sort of poems that no anthologist, no matter how silly, would think of collecting—is in a position to estimate the importance of formal technique in redeeming a poem from oblivion. A mastery of technique is rare enough in any art. But in poetry, which demands not only a superb taste in the ever-shifting symbolic system of the connotations of language and an instinct for the aesthetic significance of abstract forms and patterns, but also a deep and abiding understanding of the rhythmic psychology and even physiology of readers in general, technical mastery is not so common a gift that it appears inevitably in every generation.

It is instructive to read right through any anthology looking for some good poems—not good images, or lines, or parts, but whole poems. Most poems will exhibit little that we can admire as real formal excellence, which is to say that in few poems will both the meter and the form act as organic elements of accurate meaning. Nor should we feel pangs of shame or guilt at entertaining sharp expectations of adequacy. It is never to be forgotten that it is the business of poets to make poems, just as it is the business of readers and critics to appraise them. A young friend of Samuel Johnson's once developed feelings of shame over criticizing a tragedy when he reflected that after all he could not write a better one. Johnson responded with characteristic clarity and courage: "Why no, Sir, this is not just reasoning. You *may* abuse a tragedy, though you cannot write one. You may scold a carpenter who has made you a bad table, though you cannot make a table. It is not your trade to make tables."

We will thus not expect to find formal competence, let alone formal excellence, everywhere we turn. We will not even expect to find it in all the poems of a highly regarded poet: certain of Shakespeare's sonnets are as bad as certain of Wordsworth's failed poems; Keats does not compose brilliantly in every poem, and when Yeats is bad he is embarrassingly bad. It is our business now to supply ourselves with certain principles of excellence in stanzaic forms, never forgetting as we do so that ultimately a poem is more than its shape, important as that shape is in contributing to its totality.

One general principle with which we can begin is this: in a short multistanza poem, the poem generally tends toward a greater density the closer the number of stanzas accords with the number of divisions of action or intellection which the poem undertakes. That is, the number of stanzas into which the poem is divided should itself express something; the number should not give the impression of being accidental. Just as in, say, a successful Petrarchan sonnet the sestet offers a different kind of material from that presented in the octave because its shape and rhyme structure are different, so in poems written in either fixed or nonce stanzas separate and different shapes should embody separate and different things. Another way of saying the same thing is to suggest that the white space between stanzas means something. If nothing is conceived to be taking place within it, if no kind of silent pressure or advance or reconsideration or illumination or perception seems to be going on in that white space, the reader has a legitimate question to ask: Why is that white space there, and what am I supposed to do with it?

Thus a bipartite experience naturally calls out for expression

in two stanzas, and a tripartite experience in three. Marvell's
"To His Coy Mistress," for example, involves a tripartite rhetorical experience which is argued like a classical syllogism: (1) if
we had world enough and time, your coyness would be tolerable;
(2) we do not have sufficient world or time; (3) therefore, we
must love at a faster rate than gentility or modesty permit.
Although he has written his poem in a continuous sequence of
iambic tetrameter couplets, Marvell has separated the three elements of his argument into three indented verse-paragraphs, and,
more important, he has proportioned each according to the
logical weight of the part of the argument it embodies: the first
(the major premise) contains twenty lines, the second (the minor
premise) twelve, and the third (the conclusion) fourteen.

An even more telling way of working up a tripartite experience, this time in more complex stanzas, is exhibited in
Robert Bridges's "I Praise the Tender Flower":

> I praise the tender flower,
> That on a mournful day
> Bloomed in my garden bower
> And made the winter gay.
> Its loveliness contented
> My heart tormented.
>
> I praise the gentle maid
> Whose happy voice and smile
> To confidence betrayed
> My doleful heart awhile:
> And gave my spirit deploring
> Fresh wings for soaring.
>
> The maid for very fear
> Of love I durst not tell:
> The rose could never hear,
> Though I bespake her well:
> So in my song I bind them
> For all to find them.

The action of the whole poem consists of three sequential sub-
ordinate actions: remembrance of the flower; remembrance of
the maid; and a justification for inviting each to enter the one
poem, that is, an assertion of the poem's unity of statement. The

result is an implicit total action, an act of praise for poetry as a uniquely formal, silent way of organizing and saying. The three events in the poem remain separate until the word *So,* which introduces the final couplet: at this point the two acts of praise and the one act of reconciliatory justification become one, and this unifying act of reasoning is the logical result of the ironic contemplation that directly precedes it. If the maid had been more like the rose, or the rose more like the maid, no poem would have been necessary. Since each—although for different reasons—is inaccessible to language used normally, each becomes sufficiently like the other to justify the "binding" of the two in one poem. The white space between the first and second stanzas, that white space which is all-important in a lyric of more than one stanza, implies the question, "What else is to be praised in the same terms and structure as the flower?" The white space between the second and third stanzas implies the question, "What, after all, are this flower and this maid doing in the same poem?" To compare the final parallel couplets of each of the three stanzas is to appreciate the structural authenticity and integrity of the poem: each in turn projects the result of the action with which the stanza has been concerned.

If the poem betrays any structural fault, it lies in the greater density of the third stanza than that of the first and second: the parallelism of shapes suggests that we will be offered parallel densities, but the intellectual and emotional action that goes on in the quatrain of the final stanza proves to be of a heavier specific gravity than what we are given in the analogous part of the preceding stanzas. But if this is a structural fault, it is perhaps a fault naturally incident to a poem like this or like Marvell's "To His Coy Mistress," poems which resemble the tripartite act of the syllogism, and in which the "conclusion," because it partakes of the quality of a revelation, is naturally going to weigh more than the mere premises which precede and cause it.

Of course we would not want every lyric to exhibit the sort of absolute symmetry which "I Praise the Tender Flower" achieves. It can even be argued that the poem's symmetry and shapeliness are purchased at too high a price in the illusions of warmth and natural passion. But whether it ends as a symmetrical construct or not, we will expect every short poem to justify its

form and to lay upon its form the obligation of speaking an
appropriate part of its meaning. At the opposite pole from
Bridges's lyric we can place a poem like Norman Gale's "The
Country Faith," the three stanzas of which imply that we are
about to receive a shaped tripartite experience. But no:

> Here in the country's heart
> Where the grass is green,
> Life is the same sweet life
> As it e'er hath been.
>
> Trust in a God still lives,
> And the bell at morn
> Floats with a thought of God
> O'er the rising corn.
>
> God comes down in the rain,
> And the crop grows tall—
> This is the country faith,
> And the best of all.

Here we might contrive a reason for the space between the first
stanza and the second, but it would be hard to find one for the
space between the second and the third. This three-stanza arrangement is an example of what we can call pseudo-form.

We can apply the same designation to constructions like Oscar
Wilde's "Symphony in Yellow," whose logic is one thing and
whose tripartite form is quite another:

> An omnibus across the bridge
>   Crawls like a yellow butterfly,
>   And, here and there, a passer-by
> Shows like a little restless midge.
>
> Big barges full of yellow hay
>   Are moved against the shadowy wharf,
>   And, like a yellow silken scarf,
> The thick fog hangs along the quay.
>
> The yellow leaves begin to fade
>   And flutter from the Temple elms,
>   And at my feet the pale green Thames
> Lies like a rod of rippled jade.

We can embarrass this poem not merely by asking why it presents itself in three stanzas instead of two or four, or instead of in continuous form, but also by inquiring what is supposed to sanction the In Memoriam stanza, which is to ask what there is in the treatment of the middle two lines of each stanza that distinguishes them from the outer two. By contrast, the first stanza of Auden's "The Fall of Rome" shows how the *abba* rhyme scheme can justify itself logically:

> The piers are pummelled by the waves;
> In a lonely field the rain
> Lashes an abandoned train;
> Outlaws fill the mountain caves.

All this is not to suggest that the formality of a short poem ought to accord with some timid or reactionary convention of what organic form is: it is not to suggest that the traditional idiom of Bridges is the only one within which structural meaning can develop itself. Despite its departures from certain formal conventions, William Carlos Williams's "The Red Wheelbarrow" beautifully justifies its quadripartite form:

> so much depends
> upon
>
> a red wheel
> barrow
>
> glazed with rain
> water
>
> beside the white
> chickens.

Williams's conception is as much afflicted with the Imagist enthusiasm as Wilde's is: the difference is that Williams's poem justifies its form in its meaning, and that Wilde's does not.

Another general principle of poetic form which experience tends to confirm is this: the shorter the poem, the more perfect we expect to be its accommodation of form to its other elements. Formal perfections, indeed, bear a different relation to the whole

poem in a shorter work than they do in a longer. Every part of a
short poem is large, just as every part of a large poem is small—
just one of the occasional, tiny defects of taste in *Paradise Lost*
would sink a sonnet. We can experience this principle by looking
at a couple of poems in only two stanzas and by considering the
relation in each between shape and other elements. Consider, for
example, Margot Ruddock's "Autumn, Crystal Eye":

> Autumn, crystal eye
> Look on me,
> Passion chilled am I
> Like to thee,
>
> Seeking sterner truth,
> Even now
> Longing for the white
> Frozen bough.

What we will ask for in vain here is some sanction for the bipartite structure: actually there isn't any, and it is the more dis-
astrous that the very tininess of the poem advertises all the more
blatantly its total stanzaic form. We may contrast another poem
in two small quatrains which likewise by its very smallness and
the simplicity of its bipartite shape necessarily makes loud
structural claims. The difference is that this poem puts its money
where its mouth—or shape—is: it attains form rather than pseudo-
form, and its reward is that it has become a permanent poem. It
is Wordsworth's:

> A slumber did my spirit seal;
>   I had no human fears:
> She seem'd a thing that could not feel
>   The touch of earthly years.
>
> No motion has she now, no force;
>   She neither hears nor sees;
> Roll'd round in earth's diurnal course,
>   With rocks, and stones, and trees.

It is impossible to think of this poem's appearing in a different
structural guise, either in one continuous shape or in, say, three
or four stanzas: its action is juxtaposition or opposition; what

happens is a relation between past and present, between com-
placency and misery, illusion and reality; and the "twoness" of
the stanzas bespeaks its action. Compare what happens in the
white space between these two stanzas with what happens in the
space between Margot Ruddock's: it is the difference between
total drama and nothing at all.

But the relation between two things need not be one of opposition to justify a bipartite poetic structure. Frost's "Dust of
Snow" justifies its form by devoting one stanza to the grammatical
subject and the other to the predicate:

> The way a crow
> Shook down on me
> The dust of snow
> From a hemlock tree
>
> Has given my heart
> A change of mood
> And saved some part
> Of a day I had rued.

Another justification of a bipartite structure is the separation of
effect from cause, as in Emily Dickinson's "It Dropped So Low
in My Regard":

> It dropped so low in my regard,
> I heard it hit the ground,
> And go to pieces on the stones
> At bottom of my mind.
>
> Yet blamed the fate that fractured, less
> Than I reviled myself,
> For entertaining plated wares
> Upon my silver shelf.

But regardless of the kind of relation between the two parts,
by their shape they imply a relation that is not merely sequential.
In that relation is found the justification for the poem's appearing in the form it takes.

In more complicated stanza forms, a natural and logical deduc-
tion we should make is that units of equal size and shape imply
a degree of equality or even parallelism in the materials they

embody. In the same way, unequal lines, whether longer or shorter than their neighbors, will be expected to justify their inequality. A good example of a poem whose longer lines do so brilliantly is Hardy's "The Man He Killed." Here the general line length is trimeter, and the third line of every stanza lengthens to tetrameter. Hardy uses this stanza in a highly organic way. The moment of greatest dramatic weight—and often of grammatical weight as well—is the weightier third line of each stanza. In the first stanza, for example, although we begin in the subjunctive mode, we are shifted to indicative, independent predication at the "heavy" third line:

> "Had he and I but met
> By some old ancient inn,
> We should have sat us down to wet
> Right many a nipperkin."

A similar thing happens in the second stanza: the first independent clause in the stanza is coincident with the one longer line:

> "But ranged as infantry,
> And staring face to face,
> I shot at him as he at me,
> And killed him in his place."

In the third stanza, as the speaker begins to rationalize his intellectual and moral predicament, the weighty third line is used for the all-important repetition by which the speaker hopes to persuade himself of the reasonableness of his situation:

> "I shot him dead because—
> Because he was my foe,
> Just so: my foe of course he was;
> That's clear enough; although . . ."

The next stanza uses the long line for the speaker's important humanizing specification of the terms of his enemy's poverty:

> "He thought he'd 'list, perhaps,
> Off-hand like—just as I—
> Was out of work—had sold his traps—
> No other reason why."

And in the final stanza, his perception now as complete as it can be, and complete enough to cause the poem to conclude, the speaker uses the long line to parallel the theme of the analogous line in the first stanza: the theme of friendly pub drinking as the furthest possible antithesis to war. It is not the shooting which receives the emphasis this time: it is, ironically, the "treating":

> "Yes; quaint and curious war is!
>   You shoot a fellow down
> You'd treat if met where any bar is,
>   Or help to half a crown."

The world of difference between poetic form and poetic pseudo-form can be illustrated by William Collins's "Ode to Evening." If Hardy's "The Man He Killed" uses its stanza in a vigorously organic way, the Collins poem does not, and its failure to exploit the shape of its own stanza is probably as much a cause of its lack of permanent appeal as its more obvious defects of grandiose diction and absence of drama. Collins's stanza is an unrhymed unequal quatrain: the first two lines are iambic pentameter, the second two are iambic trimeter. The difference in weight between the two kinds of lines is even larger than in Hardy's poem; and yet Collins, apparently impervious to the implication of the shape of his stanza, neglects to exploit its opportunities for density. The third, fourth, and fifth stanzas will suffice to exhibit Collins's method:

> Now air is hushed, save where the weak-eyed bat,
> With short shrill shriek, flits by on leathern wing;
>   Or where the beetle winds
>   His small but sullen horn,
>
> As oft he rises 'midst the twilight path,
> Against the pilgrim borne in heedless hum—
>   Now teach me, maid composed,
>   To breathe some softened strain,
>
> Whose numbers, stealing through thy darkening vale,
> May not unseemly with its stillness suit,
>   As musing slow I hail
>   Thy genial loved return!

In the first of these stanzas we do see some attempt at an accommodation of the sense to the shape, although even here we cannot help noticing that the *Or* with which the beetle's action is introduced implies a parallelism with the weight of the bat's action. The difficulty is that the bat has been given eight feet whereas the equally important beetle is vouchsafed only six. But we find statement and stanzaic form really at cross-purposes in the second of the stanzas. The heart of Collins's whole poem is his prayer to Evening to grant him the power to compose a poem so "soft" and "still" that it will perfectly correspond with the thing it praises. It can be said, indeed, that what the "Ode to Evening" is about is precisely this matter of the accommodation of means to subject. But observe where Collins chooses to position this prayer. Unlike Hardy, who usually contrives that independent grammatical elements, which are naturally vigorous and emphatic, will accord with the "heavier" part of the stanza, Collins disposes his matter so that grammatical independence and emphasis will occur in exactly the "lightest" and weakest part of the stanza; he reserves the weighty, emphatic part for the much less consequential action of the beetle's behavior. The beetle, he asserts in his long lines,

> . . . rises 'midst the twilight path,
> Against the pilgrim borne in heedless hum—

and with this trivial image fully emphasized, he moves in his smaller lines to the crucial action of the poem:

> Now teach me, maid composed,
> To breathe some softened strain.

The effect is that of sending a midget to carry barbells.

Ezra Pound's remark "Poetry ought to be as well written as prose" has, to be sure, high comic value; but there is wisdom in it too. One thing it implies is that a poet should possess an instinct for rhetorical emphasis; that is, he should sense which parts of the forms he uses are naturally the appropriate vehicles of emphasis and which are not. A writer of emphatic and interesting prose, for example, is careful to place his emphatic materials in independent clauses and his less emphatic materials in dependent ones: he knows that independent clauses, which imply no need for syntactical support outside themselves, transmit an illusion of greater strength and weight. Thus instead of writing, "He was strolling along the deck when a wave washed him overboard," he writes, "While he was strolling along the deck, a wave washed him overboard." This is an elementary principle, but it is amazing how many aspirant prose writers are innocent of it.

In the same way, a writer of effective prose has mastered a general principle governing all events which occur in time, whether athletic contests, seductions, or sentences. The principle is that the middle of the event is the least interesting part, the beginning the next most interesting, and the end the most interesting. The pattern of natural emphasis in a sentence—or in any temporal unit constituting a delimited segment of time—looks like this:

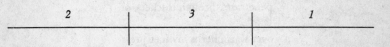

with "1" representing the most interesting moment and "3" the least. The skilled prose writer cooperates with this fact of life and makes it work on his behalf. He avoids placing the elements of the sentence in positions where they will fight against the implications of the form. Instead of saying, "He is a fool, in my opinion," he says, "He is, in my opinion, a fool."

In this one important way the poet's formal problem is very close to the prose writer's, for the poetic line, regardless of its degree of syntactical integrity, is like a prose sentence, or an opera, or a footrace in being an experience in time and in sharing in the emphasis pattern which characterizes all such experiences. Thus the part of the poetic line that is the most emphatic is the end of it: this is why end-rhyme has developed into a convention and why, say, initial rhyme has not. Rhyme is a more striking formal effect than inversion of stress: the emphasis pattern of any line helps dictate that rhyme will occur at the end and that stress inversion, a much less emphatic phenomenon, will occur most often at the beginning.

For a poet to forget—or not to know—this fact about the ends
of lines is for him to risk structural disaster the way Mortimer
Collins does in this stanza, which, despite appearances, is not
supposed to be funny:

> The oars of Ithaca dip so
> Softly into the sea,
> They waken not Calypso,
> And the hero wanders free.

Lest we imagine that this sort of thing happens at the hands
of the minor poets of the nineteenth century only, let us look
at a modern poem, "Loot," by Thom Gunn. Here are the first
three of the nine stanzas:

> I am approaching. Past dry
> towers softly seeding from mere
> delicacy of age, I
> penetrate, through thickets, or
>
> over warm herbs my feet press
> to brief potency. Now with
> the green quickness of grasses
> mingles the smell of the earth,
>
> raw and black. I am about
> to raid the earth and open
> again those low chambers that
> wary fathers stand guard in.

If Mortimer Collins is ridden by sheer ineptitude, Thom Gunn
is ridden by theory, and by theory too rigidly and insensitively applied to actualities. Mr. Gunn's decision to compose his poem
syllabically—each line contains seven syllables—unfortunately cannot repeal the psychological law of emphasis in the line.

Daniel Halpern, on the other hand, shows how it should be
done. At the beginning of his poem "Street Fire" he catches up
an important word or phrase at the end of each line, yet contrives that this artifice shall not violate his colloquial, "prose"
illusion:

It is past midnight in a thick fog when sirens
call us to the terrace.
We look down onto blossoms of bright fire
opening from manholes on Fifth Avenue.
There are men standing and smoking in rubber jackets
outside a garment district café,
the lights fluttering, the fire
offering us its electric smoke.

Every part of a poetic line accumulates weight progressively: every part anticipates the end of the line. This is less because the line is positioned in a poem than because the line is a unit of measured time. Even if the end of the line offers us no rhyme to signal the fruition of the accumulation, the end of the line constitutes an accumulation of forces, and for Mr. Gunn to position his modifiers, conjunctions, prepositions, and similar unemphatic syntactical elements at the ends of the lines is for him to fight against the nature of his chosen form. Indeed, his inattention to the natural emphasis pattern of the line seems a corollary of a larger structural insensitivity: we will surely inquire long before we discover the principle of stanzaic division in "Loot."

In matters of emphasis, then, we find it all too true that poetry should be at least as well written as prose. But the poet's formal problem, although in one way resembling the prose writer's, is infinitely more complex: while the prose writer is adjusting his matter to only one "stanza form"—the sentence—the poet must be a master not only of this form but, simultaneously, of another as well, his chosen stanzaic or stichic form, which constantly cuts across sentence structure and which unremittingly invites him to attain a triumph, like Hardy's, or to risk a disaster, like Collins's. When we realize that a lifetime is quite insufficient for the achievement of even a prose style that is fully emphatic and always weighted just right, we can appreciate the almost insuperable obstacles that the poet has elected to encounter. We can then value correctly his very occasional hard-won masterpieces.

With Collins's and Gunn's structural miscarriages we can contrast the witty and fully expressive use of stanzaic form in

something like Francis Bacon's *"In vitam humanam,"* a poem in
four eight-line stanzas. We can appreciate his second line fully
by recalling that a *span* is a measure of spatial distance—the distance between the tip of the thumb and the tip of the little
finger when the hand is fully extended: line 2 measures this distance in its size as well as in its statement:

> The world's a bubble, and the life of man
>   Less than a span;
> In his conception wretched, and from the womb
>   So to the tomb;
> Curst from the cradle, and brought up to years
>   With cares and fears.
> Who then to frail mortality shall trust
> But limns the water, or but writes in dust.

The principle of formal parallelism beautifully operates in the
short lines here: once the shortness of the experience contained
in the short lines has been emphasized by line 2, we associate the
experiences implied by lines 4 and 6 likewise with brevity. All
these short, light lines are preparing us for the contrast of the
mighty weight of the concluding couplet, the heaviest part of
the stanza structurally, and exploited by Bacon so that it becomes
the weightiest part—that is, the conclusion, introduced by *then*
—of the argument as well. We notice too that it is only the
concluding couplet that is wholly independent and complete
grammatically: it is the only predication in the poem which
elides no verbs. The student of the semantics and logic of rhymes
can profit from considering the kinds of literal and ironic meaning that are generated from such sound resemblances as *man-
span; womb-tomb; years-fears;* and *trust-dust.* Bacon's use of the
shape of his stanza has resulted in an impressive density, the sort
of density that we can never really exhaust.

There would seem to be something about the Renaissance
poet's contemplation of human mortality that urges him to his
most sensitive perceptions of the weight of stanzaic elements.
Consider not merely Bacon but Herrick, whose "To Daffodils"
performs its bipartite action with an equally exquisite structural
taste:

Fair daffodils, we weep to see
   You haste away so soon;
As yet the early-rising sun
   Has not attained his noon.
     Stay, stay,
    Until the hasting day
     Has run
   But to the even-song;
And, having prayed together, we
   Will go with you along.

We have short time to stay, as you;
   We have as short a spring,
As quick a growth to meet decay,
   As you, or anything.
     We die
   As your hours do, and dry
     Away
   Like to the summer's rain;
Or as the pearls of morning's dew,
   Ne'er to be found again.

The first monometer line ("Stay, stay") to which the stanza soon diminishes establishes an irony which the subsequent monometers will echo and parallel. The irony generated from this first monometer results from the opposition between the brevity of the line, on the one hand, and, on the other, the hopes for longevity expressed by the speaker. It is as if the very line length were exposing the hopelessness of his apostrophe to the daffodils. In the same way, the second monometer ("Has run") implies by its length the shortness of the day whose course is a hasty running rather than a more ample and leisurely movement. By the time we arrive at the second stanza, we have come to expect that the monometers will enact ideas of brevity. Thus "We die" says much more than its statement: it says, "We die rapidly." Or "We die so soon that we have no extra time or space." The actual length of the lines becomes an indispensable element of meaning.

The contribution of line length to meaning is a phenomenon which underlies a whole tradition of exotic "shaped" poems: the formal name of such a poem is *Carmen figuratum*. The most famous of these is perhaps George Herbert's "Easter Wings,"

where the implications of the statement diminish as the lines
shorten, and expand as the lines lengthen:

> Lord, who createdst man in wealth and store,
>   Though foolishly he lost the same,
>   Decaying more and more
>   Till he became
>   Most poor;
>   With thee
>   Oh, let me rise
>   As larks, harmoniously,
>   And sing this day thy victories;
> Then shall the fall further the flight in me.
>
> My tender age in sorrow did begin;
>   And still with sickness and shame
>   Thou didst so punish sin,
>   That I became
>   Most thin.
>   With thee
>   Let me combine,
>   And feel this day thy victory,
>   For if I imp my wing on thine,
> Affliction shall advance the flight in me.

This is of course very witty, but like most shaped poems it incurs
one important artistic disadvantage: it makes an unbalanced
sensuous appeal—its structure directs itself more to the eye than
to the ear. Indeed, to appreciate the wit fully, to perceive the
shape of these angels' wings, we must at some point turn the
page sideways and give ourselves up to an exercise in visual perception which belongs to the graphic rather than to the temporal
arts. Our eyes admire, but we are left with the feeling that the
visual experience of the stanzas has triumphed inharmoniously
over their auditory appeal. Or better, we feel that the two dimensions are not married: one is simply in command of the
other.

   The same weakness of an unbalanced appeal and hence a dis-
unified experience attaches, but perhaps less strongly, to John
Hollander's "For a Thirtieth Birthday, with a Bottle of Bur-
gundy":

                    Drop by
                    Drop it
                    Empties
                    Now not
                    Even as
                    Our own
                    Tearful
                    Vintage
                   Gathering
                  Itself with
                 Such slowness
                Gradually might
              Widen at the bottom
              Of some oblate vessel
              But as when the pouring
            Bottle now nearly half of
            Its old wine spent delivers
            The rest up in sobs rapidly
            Tears years and wine expire
            As tosspot Time sends after
            His cellerer once more alas
            Then let the darkling drops
            Wept in a decent year along
            The golden slopes elude for
            A moment or so his horribly
            Steady pouring hand and run
            Into sparkling glasses still
            Unshattered yes and undimmed.

The trouble here is that once we are past the middle of the
bottle, up to which point we have delighted to participate in the
"gradually widening" sense and shape, our pleasures of dual perception are largely at an end. The poem has difficulty sustaining
itself on its own terms once it passes the crucial point of its visual
wit; Mr. Hollander's lees are no more exciting than real ones.

Perhaps the greatest limitation of shaped poems like these
is the scarcity of visual objects which they can imitate: their
shapes can reflect the silhouettes of wings, bottles, hourglasses,
and altars, but where do we go from there? The art of *Carmen
figuratum* is the province perhaps more of the typographer, who
works primarily in one sense dimension, than of the poet, who
must exactly interfuse two. It is in the delicacy of this joint

appeal to eye and ear at once, it is in the perfect harmony of the address to visual and auditory logic at the same time, that any poem achieves its triumphs, and with its triumphs, its permanence.

There are many reasons why a poem has the power to endure, to transcend its own local, historical moment and to join itself to the very small body of permanent work which calls us back to it again and again. One of the foremost reasons for a poem's powers of endurance is its structural integrity, the sort of logical accommodation of statement to form, of elements to wholes, that we have been considering. Although successful poems do not always inhabit a world of logic, their forms do; and just as the world of logic is constructed from immutable propositions, so those elements of poems which belong to that world partake of immutability. Like the forms of geometry or music, the forms of poetry, whether stichic or strophic, fixed or occasional, attach the art of poetry to a permanent world—that is, they effect this attachment if they are sufficiently logical, economical, and organic.

It is interesting to notice, finally, that poems in traditional formal structures all the way from Shakespeare's sonnets to Yeats's "Sailing to Byzantium" seem to concern themselves with something like a traditional subject-matter—namely, the menace of mutability, formlessness, flux, or dissolution. This is to suggest that there is an essential poemly theme, one invited into poems by the formal preoccupations of the traditional poet. The poet organizing thought and feeling into stanzaic shapes is performing the technical corollary of what will be found to be most often his theme: permanence at war with the temporary, timelessness struggling with time, life opposing death.

10

Conventions
and the Individual Talent

To probe into the technical and mechanical operations by which any art attains its ends often distresses people who adhere to romantic and vitalistic theories of aesthetics and of the literary process. To such people the very term "convention" will carry largely pejorative implications, suggesting an insipid dependence on the modes of the past; an unquestioning acceptance of the value of artistic restraint; and a mechanical—even automatic and wholly thoughtless—repetition of "unnatural" or "artificial" literary kinds and techniques. When such people refer to an artist as conventional, they do not mean to praise him. When such people speak of literary conventions, they do so to suggest that it is time for the conventions to be overthrown. The idea of conventions and the conventional thus suggests images of a shriveled orthodoxy, of a reactionary obsession with past usages which is necessarily at war with "originality," with "freedom," with "naturalness," and with "invention."

But to those perhaps of a more empirical cast of mind, the term "convention" suggests none of these unhappy implications. To these people, art is not nature and never can be: all art must be "nature methodized" by some agreed-upon symbols if it is to be recognized as "art" by the audience. No matter how enthusiastic our adherence to "the natural," when we see a play we are not scandalized to behold the furniture all facing unnaturally toward

the audience; when we look at a painting, we are not jolted
when we perceive that we are being asked to imagine three
dimensions in the two-dimensional; when we look at a piece of
sculpture, we are not offended that the flesh, instead of resembling flesh, looks like granite or marble, or stainless steel. These
are some of the obvious conventions of these arts, and these conventions originate in the fact of the very artificiality of art. A
stage is not a room, and we know it; a painting is not three-
dimensional; granite is not like flesh. The way art works is to
transfer the experience of one sense or psychological dimension
to that of another, and it can perform this act of transference only
by means of elaborate and relatively fixed conventions which
have been found appropriate to a given kind of art. All this is
to say that art works by artifice, by illusion, and by technique,
and that no amount of talent, idea, or largeness of soul or heart
in the artist produces anything except through artifice or technique, through, that is, a mastery of the conventions appropriate
to the art.

The audience at a film unconsciously knows the technical
cinematic conventions so well that it would be puzzled if asked
to articulate them and would reject attempts to alter them.
The audience's acceptance of a rapid series of static, still pictures
as an illusion of sequential motion is perhaps the primary convention of the cinema. Another is that a sudden cut from one
scene to another betokens a strict sequence in time. A dissolve
from one scene into another is read conventionally by the audience to mean that the second scene is taking place simultaneously
with the first. A fade-out followed by a fade-in is a conventional
technique for communicating the illusion of a considerable lapse
of time. We would be lost and frustrated if the cinema abandoned
these technical conventions. And we do not regard these conventions as somehow interfering with the cinema's portrayal of a
coherent image of reality, but just the opposite: they are, we
realize, the very means by which the film renders an account of
time and action that we recognize as artistically meaningful.
These conventions do not restrain expression: they make it
possible. Far from curbing creativity, they release it.

Conventions like these are not something imported from outside and laid over art: they are inseparable elements of every act
of art. As Harry Levin has said in his essay "Notes on Conven-

tion," the very concept of artistic convention "traces its origin to imperfection—not to the fault of the craftsman, but to the limitation of the craft. Since art never imitates nature quite perfectly, there must be a margin of error: an allowance for unnaturalness, a residue of artificiality." Conventions are so inseparably a part of the act of art that we are not really presented with a choice of using them or not: the only choice we are offered is that of using them skillfully or clumsily, significantly or meaninglessly. And there is no source of conventions inside ourselves: they reside only in public places, only in external history—for a convention is a symbol of a public agreement between artist and audience that certain kinds of artificiality will be not only accepted but actually relished as pertaining to the essence of the art. As Levin has said, "A private convention, like a prefabricated myth, is a contradiction in terms."

What, then, are the conventions of poetry? Those that concern us here are the prosodic conventions, the artificialities of meter, rhyme, stanza, and—perhaps the most unnatural of all—logical rhetorical organization. This last is indeed highly artificial and conventional, for when we speak not in poems but "naturally" or colloquially, we do not usually take care to organize what we are uttering logically: we speak not in paragraphs but in bursts. We do not conduct a discourse: we make remarks. And as Gertrude Stein once reminded Hemingway, "Ernest, remarks are not literature." What makes the writing of even good prose so difficult is that its conventions of logic, coherence, emphasis, and economy are so unnatural to us. And if prose writing is difficult because it is so unnatural, we can sense the infinitely larger world of artificiality in which a poet works, even when he would disarm us by asserting that he is writing "In a Country Churchyard" or "On a Seat by a Yew Tree." Actually, poems are written not in the great outdoors where papers blow about and where one has no access to dictionaries, but at desks; their rhythms come as often from other poems as from the pulses of the poet; their stanzas are more frequently given the poet by history than supplied by momentary inspiration; and their varieties of logical organization are as artificial and labored over as the cornice of a stone building, or the nose of a statue in porphyry. As Northrop Frye writes in *Anatomy of Criticism:* "It is hardly possible to accept a critical view which . . . imagines that a 'creative' poet sits down with a pencil and some blank paper and eventually produces a new poem in a special act of creation *ex nihilo.* Human beings do not create in that way. . . . Literature may have life, reality, experience, nature, imaginative truth, social conditions, or what you will for its *content;* but literature itself is not made out of these things. Poetry can only be made out of other poems . . . the *forms* of literature can no more exist outside literature than the forms of sonata and fugue and rondo can exist outside music." And emphasizing the empirical check on all literary theorizing, he concludes: "The notion that convention shows a lack of feeling, and that a poet attains 'sincerity' . . . by disregarding [convention], is opposed to all the facts of literary experience and history."

It was T. S. Eliot, in his essay "Tradition and the Individual Talent," which appeared sixty years ago, who was among the first to remind us of the indispensable role of history and tradition in the creation of any new work of art, and who reminded us also of the necessary objectivity of the work of art. "The emotion of art is impersonal," says Eliot. "And the poet cannot reach this impersonality without surrendering himself wholly to the work to be done." As we saw at the beginning, "the work to be done," at least if we are to credit Auden and Eliot when they report as practitioners of their art, is a work more prosodic and technical than we might imagine. It is the work of knowing the prosodic conventions and of manipulating them so as to induce appropriate responses and illusions in an audience that knows them too. The individual talent is speechless without the conventions. And without an almost equal understanding of them, the audience, for all its intelligence and good will, hears nothing.

Frank Kermode has summed up E. H. Gombrich's theory of visual art this way: "The innocent eye sees nothing." As he explains: "We see what, in one way or another, we are disposed to see. What disposes us may be in some degree biological, but it is primarily cultural; what we see is what tradition enables us to see." And he continues: "Symbols, like signals, are meaningless outside some determining context, some accepted scale or structure of significations. We learn these structures, perhaps merely by our education within a particular culture, perhaps because we grow familiar with a particular convention or because a particular artist teaches us to recognize them in his own colors, tones, or themes. Until we are disposed to detect these structures our eye or ear remains innocent. Neither expression nor communication is possible in an unstructured medium."

Now we can say that what poetic fixed forms do is to supply the equivalent in poetry of these structures of signification that Kermode speaks of. Expression and a degree of communication can, perhaps, take place in "an unstructured medium," but poetic expression and communication cannot. Poetic meters and forms are the conventions through which poetry works. The poet expresses himself by reflecting his uniqueness off the solid back-board, as it were, of the conventional. Without the presence of the conventional to be new-shaped by the individual talent, the talent loses the power of transmitting its individuality. What happens in all art is, in Gombrich's words, an "interdependence of expression and tradition."

This relation between the conventions of poetry and the in-dividual talent we can scrutinize by turning now from generaliza-tions to an actual poem. Here is one by Donald Justice, "In Bertram's Garden":

> Jane looks down at her organdy skirt
> As if *it* somehow were the thing disgraced,
> For being there, on the floor, in the dirt,
> And she catches it up about her waist,
> Smooths it out along one hip,
> And pulls it over the crumpled slip.
>
> On the porch, green-shuttered, cool,
> Asleep is Bertram, that bronze boy,
> Who, having wound her around a spool,
> Sends her spinning like a toy
> Out to the garden, all alone,
> To sit and weep on a bench of stone.
>
> Soon the purple dark will bruise
> Lily and bleeding-heart and rose,
> And the little Cupid lose
> Eyes and ears and chin and nose,
> And Jane lie down with others soon
> Naked to the naked moon.

There are infinite ways of enacting the general theme of loss of innocence, but the conventions finely assist Justice to attain his enactment. We can consider, first of all, the stanza and its associations. It is a stanza consisting of a tetrameter quatrain and a couplet, and we have met it before: in Wordsworth's "I Wandered Lonely as a Cloud." The stanza is, indeed, firmly associated with that poem, and for Justice to use it for his horrid little erotic melodrama is for him to extend his irony and deepen his horror. Contemplating his daffodils, Wordsworth says:

> A poet could not but be gay,
> In such a jocund company.

Justice overtly says nothing about his attitude toward what he oversees. But his stanza, and the ironies it develops, implies worlds of emotion and volumes of personal commentary.

The conventional accumulation of weight at the ends of lines in stanzas assists both Justice and the reader to schematize the experience with an economy amounting to the laconic. Just to run down the right-hand side of the poem and to pronounce the rhymes alone is to trace something like the action of the poem: we could surely deduce a seduction from *skirt, disgraced, dirt, waist, hip, slip;* and a scheme of coition and postcoital lassitude from *cool, boy, spool, toy, alone, stone;* and perhaps even a sense of the darkened knowledge which time will offer Jane in *bruise, rose, lose, nose, soon, moon.* And the convention that the terminal position in the line is the all-important one is what, in line 11, gives the words *all alone,* words which stand as the very emblem of Jane's new world of experience, such force that they almost knock us down.

The convention of rhyme appears to function here, as it very frequently does, not as a curb upon invention but rather as an active stimulator of it. Consider the first four lines of the second stanza:

> On the porch, green-shuttered, cool,
> Asleep is Bertram, that bronze boy,
> Who, having wound her around a spool,
> Sends her spinning like a toy. . . .

It seems very likely that a poet working without rhyme would have had Bertram send Jane into the garden "spinning like a top": there is nothing but the conventional stricture of rhyme to transform the thing set spinning from a top, which we would expect, into a "toy," which we do not expect, but which proves to be perfect. "Toy" prevents the idea of the toy top ever to vanish entirely from our imagery, while at the same time it implies the appropriate ideas of condescension, victimization, and triviality. Jane, after all, has been toyed with, in several senses, and is finally reduced to a mechanical plaything: she is like the victim of the "young man carbuncular" in "The Waste Land," the girl who after the act smooths her hair with a hand as automatic and mechanical as that which Jane uses to smooth her "disgraced" organdy skirt. And Jane's physical behavior in the first stanza echoes also Eliot's account in "Sweeney Among the Nightingales" of the mechanical actions of "the person in the Spanish cape," who

> Tries to sit on Sweeney's knees
>
> Slips and pulls the table cloth
> Overturns a coffee-cup,
> Reorganized upon the floor
> She yawns and draws a stocking up.

Sweeney and Bertram share more than boredom and sexual contempt: they share a conventional meter, and it is Justice's management of Eliot's meter which first sets these rich echoes reverberating.

The metrical convention adds further density to the proceedings. The meter of the poem is rising four-stress accentual, with the number of syllables per line varying from seven to ten. The base iambic-anapestic meter is here the equivalent of the "structured medium" of which Kermode speaks: it is the only thing that makes rhythmical meaning possible. We can consider, for example, the rhythmical treatment of line 8, the line which introduces us to the exhausted and no longer interested Bertram. By inverting the syntax of the initial clause and writing "Asleep is Bertram" rather than "Bertram is asleep," Justice avoids an initial trochee and establishes instead a two-foot sequence of iambic rhythm as a preparation for the pressure of the surprising spondee "bronze boy," a spondee whose rhythmical force is an accurate corollary and cause of our surprise at the image. In a similar way, initial trochees, which would be meaningless unless positioned against the structure of the conventional iambic medium, do their work of reinforcement, make their contribution to the density of texture. In the final two lines, for example, the jolting initial trochee "Naked" arrives with the greater force for appearing only after six iambic feet have prepared for it. Those who speak of the "tyranny" of the iambic foot might speak just as well of the tyranny of friction which enables us to run, or the tyranny of gravity which permits dancing and high-jumping to differ beautifully from walking.

But perhaps the most conspicuous conventional element in Justice's poem is the use of stanzaic divisions to enact logical shifts in focus. The first stanza holds us firmly within the present time, and prepares us to ask the question which the white space implies: "What has happened?" In answering that question, the second stanza executes a subtle shift of time, beginning in present, shifting to past, and returning to present. The white space between the second stanza and the last asks its own logical question: "What will happen?" And the last stanza, like a perfectly drilled clairvoyant, penetrates into the future both of the oncoming evening and of the oncoming darkness and repetitiveness which will be Jane's experience. It is the very precision of this structure that generates the pathos; it is exactly this tight control that releases the horror. By dividing Jane's experience in this precise tripartite way, Justice is enabled to scrutinize it, and the one thing that it cannot stand is scrutiny. The poem's moral awareness is implied covertly by the exactitude of its shape. Again we see that, far from constraining the individual talent, the conventions have permitted the poet to see what it is that he means, to hear what his own voice is saying, and to realize what is in the materials he has before him. It is the conventions that enable him to see, and to hear, and to think poetically. And it is the reader's comfort within the conventions that makes it possible for the poem to transmit its signals at all.

"The innocent eye sees nothing." The unwitting reader finds poems "obscure." It is the trained reader alone who fits himself for that great repeated act of complicity with the poet which is the source of the fullest delight and the fullest enlightenment; for the reader is an individual talent too, and it is technical knowledge and command that release his own singular energies and open for him his own liberating vision.

Suggestions for Further Reading

Chatman, Seymour, *A Theory of Meter* (The Hague, 1965). "An attempt to demonstrate the utility of structural linguistics in developing a theory of English meter."

Cunningham, J. V., *Collected Essays* (Chicago, 1977). The essays on "Tradition and Poetic Structure" are especially to the point.

Frye, Northrop, *Anatomy of Criticism* (Princeton, 1957), pp. 251–62. Twelve pages of acute remarks and telling examples of the expressive uses of metrical variations, especially in Spenser.

Fuller, John, *The Sonnet* (London, 1972). A brief but clear and interesting treatment, with bibliography.

Fussell, Paul, *Theory of Prosody in Eighteenth-Century England* (New London, Conn., 1954). An introduction to some of the difficulties and implications of metrical description.

Gross, Harvey, *Sound and Form in Modern Poetry: A Study of Prosody from Thomas Hardy to Robert Lowell* (Ann Arbor, 1964). A bright, clear, and engaging account of modern prosodic practice, with emphasis on Marianne Moore, W. C. Williams, Cummings, Pound, Eliot, Hart Crane, Auden, Roethke, and Dylan Thomas.

Gross, Harvey, ed., *The Structure of Verse: Modern Essays on Prosody* (New York, 1966). Fifteen essays by scholars, critics, and poets, including Robert Graves, Ezra Pound, and (especially valuable) Theodore Roethke.

Harding, D. W., *Words into Rhythm: English Speech Rhythm in Verse and Prose* (Cambridge, 1976). Contentious but provocative speculations by a literary psychologist.

Hollander, John, *Vision and Resonance: Two Senses of Poetic Form* (New York, 1975). Twelve shrewd and learned essays on meter and form and prosodic theory illuminated by a scholar's awareness of history and a poet's taste.

Malof, Joseph, "The Native Rhythm of English Meters," *University of Texas Studies in Literature and Language*, V (1964), pp. 580–94, Argues that one source of metrical interest in the English line is the recurrent encounter between the native four-stress tradition and numerous foreign, imported metrical conventions.

National Poetry Festival Held in the Library of Congress, October 22-24, 1962: Proceedings (Washington, 1964). Full of technical observations by contemporary poets. The remarks on "The Problem of Form" by Leonie Adams and J. V. Cunningham are especially illuminating.

Omond, T. S., *English Metrists* (Oxford, 1921). A survey of metrical theory from 1545 through the nineteenth century. Indispensable for bibliography.

Preminger, Alex, Frank J. Warnke, and O. B. Hardison, Jr., eds., *Princeton Encyclopedia of Poetry and Poetics* (Princeton, 1965; enlarged edition, 1974). A comprehensive dictionary of critical and technical terms encountered in the discussion of poetry.

Ransom, John Crowe, *The New Criticism* (Norfolk, Va., 1941). Chapter 4 ("Wanted: An Ontological Critic") considers the intercourse between meter and statement as central to the uniqueness of poetry.

Richards, I. A., *Practical Criticism: A Study of Literary Judgment* (New York, 1929). A salutary exhibition of—among other things—the cost of metrical misapprehensions.

Richards, I. A., *Principles of Literary Criticism* (New York, 1928). Chapter 17 contains suggestive observations on the psychological and physiological effects of meter on the reader.

Saintsbury, George, *A History of English Prosody from the Twelfth Century to the Present Day* (New York, 1906–10; 3 vols.) Old-fashioned in taste, but a classic. Indispensable for beginners.

Shapiro, Karl, and Robert Beum, *A Prosody Handbook* (New York, 1965). A standard descriptive work with an extensive bibliography.

Thompson, John, *The Founding of English Metre* (New York, 1961). An acute analysis of Renaissance metrical theory and practice from Wyatt to Sidney.

Wimsatt, W. K., Jr., "One Relation of Rhyme to Reason," in *The Verbal Icon: Studies in the Meaning of Poetry* (Lexington, Ky., 1954). On the relation between rhyme sounds and the structures of logical meaning.

Wimsatt, W. K., Jr., and Monroe C. Beardsley, "The Concept of Meter: An Exercise in Abstraction," in Wimsatt, *Hateful Contraries: Studies in Literature and Criticism* (Lexington, Ky., 1965). A defense of the "homely and sound, traditional and objective principles of prosody" against the attacks of linguists and musical scansionists.

Wimsatt, W. K., Jr., ed., *Versification: Major Language Types* (New York, 1972). Essays by sixteen authors on the prosodies of various languages ancient and modern. Contains an excellent critical bibliography (by Rae Ann Nager) of writings on English prosody.

Index

alexandrine, 48, 125, 132, 147

Allen, Donald M., 150

Ammons, A. R., 89; *Corson's Inlet*, 82–83

anaphora, 80

Aristotle, 12, 98

Arnold, Matthew, 72; *Dover Beach*, 33–34, 52

Ascham, Roger, 68

Auden, W. H., 3, 7, 73, 80, 145, 153, 176; *The Age of Anxiety*, 65; *The Fall of Rome*, 54, 159; *In Memory of W. B. Yeats*, 54; *September 1, 1939*, 9–10, 58

Bacon, Francis, *In vitam humanam*, 168

ballad stanza, 63, 66, 133–4, 150

Barker, George, *Memorial*, 99

Battle of Maldon, 24, 62

Beardsley, Monroe, 32, 64

Beerbohm, Max, 98

Bell, Marvin, *Here*, 82

Bentley, Edmund Clerihew, 138–9

Bentley, Richard, 69–70

Beowulf, 63–64

Bidlake, John, *The Country Parson*, 92

Blackmur, R. P., *Mr. Virtue and the Three Bears*, 145

Blake, William, 78; *The Chimney Sweeper (Songs of Innocence)*,

15–16; *Mock On, Mock On*, 47; *The Sick Rose*, 103–4; *Songs of Innocence and Experience*, 3

Bly, Robert, 81, 84

Boswell, James, 4

Bridges, Robert, 16, 158; *Cheddar Pinks*, 7–8; *I Praise the Tender Flower*, 156–7; *Wintry Delights*, 11–12

Brinnin, John Malcolm, 149

Brooks, Cleanth, 4

Browning, Robert, *Fra Lippo Lippi*, 43, 49, 71; *Love among the Ruins*, 91; *My Last Duchess*, 129; *The Statue and the Bust*, 132

Burns, Robert, *The Cotter's Saturday Night*, 148; *Epistle to John Lapraik*, 144–5; *The Holy Fair*, 144; *Holy Willie's Prayer*, 143; *To a Mountain Daisy*, 143

Buson, Taniguchi, 133

Butler, Samuel, *Hudibras*, 130

Byron, George Gordon, Lord, *Don Juan*, 146–7

Bysshe, Edward, 69

caesura, 23–26, 65, 67

Campion, Thomas, 3, 68

Carmen figuratum, 169–72

Catullus, 136

Chapman, George, 117